**TEACHER'S PET PUBLICATIONS**

PUZZLE PACK
for
Night

based on the book by
Elie Wiesel

Written by
Mary B. Collins

© 2005 Teacher's Pet Publications
All Rights Reserved

The materials in this packet are copyrighted
by Teacher's Pet Publications, Inc.

These pages may be duplicated by the purchaser
for use in the purchaser's own classroom.

Copying any of these materials and distributing them
for any other purpose is a violation of the copyright laws.

© 2005 Teacher's Pet Publications, Inc.
www.tpet.com

INTRODUCTION
If you already own the LitPlan for this title, this Puzzle Pack will refresh your Unit Resource Materials and Vocabulary Resource Materials sections plus give you additional materials you can substitute into the tests. If you do not already have a complete LitPlan, these pages will give you some supplemental materials to use with your own plan. There are two main groups of materials: one set for unit words (such as characters' names, symbols, places, etc.) and one set for vocabulary words associated with the book.

WORD LIST
There is a word list for both the unit words and the vocabulary words. These lists show you which words are being used in the materials and the clues or definitions being used for those words. You may want to give students a word list with clues/definitions to help them, or you may want students to only have a word list (without clues/definitions) if you want them to work a little harder. Both are available for duplication. The word lists can also be your "calling key" for the bingo games.

FILL IN THE BLANK AND MATCHING
There are 4 each of the fill in the blank and matching worksheets for both the unit and vocabulary words. These pages can be used either as extra worksheets for students or as objective parts of a unit test. They can be done individually if students need extra help or as a whole class activity to review the material covered.

MAGIC SQUARES
The magic squares not only reinforce the material covered but also work on reasoning and math skills. Many teachers have told us that their students really enjoy doing these!

WORD SEARCH PUZZLES
The word search words go in all directions, as indicated on your answer keys. Two of the word search puzzles have the clues listed rather than the words. This makes the puzzle a little more difficult, but it reinforces the material better. Two word search puzzles have words only for students who find the clue puzzles too difficult.

CROSSWORD PUZZLES
Both unit and vocabulary word sections have 4 crossword puzzles.

BINGO CARDS
There are 32 individual bingo cards for the unit words and 32 individual bingo cards for the vocabulary words. You can use your word list as a "call list," calling the words at random and marking them off of your list as you go, or you could use the flash cards by cutting them apart and drawing the words at random from a hat (or box or whatever). To make a better review, you might ask for the definition and spelling of each word as you call it out–or you could call out the definitions and have students tell you the words they need to look for on the puzzle.

JUGGLE LETTERS
The vocabulary juggle letter game is intended to help students learn the spellings of the words. One sheet has the definitions listed on it as an extra help for students who need it or to reinforce the definitions if you choose to do so.

FLASH CARDS
We've included a set of vocabulary flash cards you can duplicate, cut, and fold for your students. Some teachers make a few sets for general use by the class; others make a set for each student. Some teachers duplicate them for each student and have the students cut & fold their own. You can cut out just the words and put them in a hat, have each student pick out one word and write the definition and a sentence for that word. Students then swap words and papers, with the next student adding a sentence of his own under the last one. You can have students swap as many times as you like. Each time the student will read the sentences written prior to his own and then add a sentence. You can cut out the words and definitions separately and play "I Have; Who Has?" Each student in the room draws a word and definition. The first student says, "I have (the name of the word). Who has the definition?" The student with the definition reads it then says, "I have (the name of the vocabulary word she has). Who has the definition?" The round continues until all words and definitions have been given.

Night Word List

No.	Word	Clue/Definition
1.	ALPHONSE	The German Jew who headed the block at Buna
2.	AMERICAN	An ___ tank was at the gates of Buchenwald
3.	AUSCHWITZ	Had a sign that said "Work is liberty!"
4.	BEA	The next eldest of the Wiesel children
5.	BEETHOVEN	Jewish musicians were not allowed to play this composer's music
6.	BIRKENAU	The reception center for Auschwitz
7.	BREAD	The prisoners ate this and soup
8.	BUCHENWALD	Mr. Wiesel died in this camp
9.	BUNA	They walked here from Auschwitz
10.	CHLOMO	Elie's father's first name
11.	CLEAN	The men had to ___ the block before they evacuated
12.	DRUMER	Akiba ___ thought God was testing the Jews
13.	DYING	This idea began to fascinate Elie during the evacuation
14.	DYSENTERY	Mr. Wiesel had this ailment when he died
15.	ELIAHOU	The Rabbi ___ was looking for his son
16.	ELIE	The only son
17.	FASCISTS	They attacked Jewish shops and synagogues
18.	FAST	Elie did not do this on Yom Kippur
19.	FOOT	Elie had surgery on his ___
20.	FRANEK	He tormented Elie's father to get Elie's gold tooth
21.	GESTAPO	The German security police
22.	GHETTOS	Two ___ were set up in Sighet
23.	GLEIWITZ	The marchers' destination
24.	HILDA	The eldest of the Wiesel children
25.	HITLER	One Jew said he was the only one who had kept his promises
26.	HOSPITAL	Elie and his father did not stay here, but joined the evacuation
27.	HUNGARIAN	Elie hated these police first
28.	IDEK	The Kapo who had bouts of madness
29.	JULIEK	Played his violin for the dying men
30.	KADDISH	The men recited this prayer for themselves
31.	KATZ	Meir ___ died in the wagon
32.	KIPPUR	The Day of Atonement: Yom ___
33.	MARTHA	Offered the family safe refuge in her village
34.	MENGELE	Elie saw this notorious doctor
35.	MOSHE	He tried to warn the Jews in Sighet: ___ the Beadle
36.	PALESTINE	Elie wanted his family to move here
37.	PASSOVER	The Germans arrested the Jewish leaders on the seventh day of ___
38.	RESISTANCE	This movement rescued the prisoners at Buchenwald
39.	ROSH	The Jewish New Year: ___ Hashanah
40.	RUSSIANS	They liberated the men in the hospital
41.	SCHACHTER	Woman who had a vision of the furnaces
42.	SELECTION	It was the gravest danger
43.	SIGHET	Elie Wiesel grew up in this town
44.	SNOWED	It ___ during the entire evacuation march
45.	SOUP	It once tasted like corpses
46.	SPOON	Elie's inheritance was a knife and a ___
47.	STAR	Jews had to wear the yellow ___
48.	STEIN	Mr. Wiesel didn't recognize this cousin
49.	STERN	A tradesman turned policeman
50.	TIBI	Dreamed of going to Haifa with Elie and Yossi

Copyrighted

Night Word List Continued

No.	Word	Clue/Definition
51.	TRANSYLVANIA	The country where Elie Wiesel grew up
52.	TZIPORA	The youngest of the Wiesel children
53.	VIOLIN	It was crushed along with Juliek
54.	YOSSI	Told Elie he had not been written down
55.	ZALMAN	A Polish boy who was trampled during the evacuation

Night Fill In The Blank 1

_____ 1. Elie Wiesel grew up in this town

_____ 2. Mr. Wiesel died in this camp

_____ 3. One Jew said he was the only one who had kept his promises

_____ 4. He tried to warn the Jews in Singhet: ___ the Beadle

_____ 5. Elie had surgery on his ___

_____ 6. The country where Elie Wiesel grew up

_____ 7. Mr. Wiesel didn't recognize this cousin

_____ 8. Elie saw this notorious doctor

_____ 9. The youngest of the Wiesel children

_____ 10. The eldest of the Wiesel children

_____ 11. Dreamed of going to Haifa with Elie and Yossi

_____ 12. The marchers' destination

_____ 13. An ___ tank was at the gates of Buchenwald

_____ 14. Mr. Wiesel had this ailment when he died

_____ 15. They liberated the men in the hospital

_____ 16. Two ___ were set up in Sighet

_____ 17. Had a sign that said "Work is liberty!"

_____ 18. The Germans arrested the Jewish leaders on the seventh day of ___

_____ 19. Offered the family safe refuge in her village

_____ 20. They attacked Jewish shops and synagogues

Night Fill In The Blank 1 Answer Key

SIGHET	1. Elie Wiesel grew up in this town
BUCHENWALD	2. Mr. Wiesel died in this camp
HITLER	3. One Jew said he was the only one who had kept his promises
MOSHE	4. He tried to warn the Jews in Singhet: ___ the Beadle
FOOT	5. Elie had surgery on his ___
TRANSYLVANIA	6. The country where Elie Wiesel grew up
STEIN	7. Mr. Wiesel didn't recognize this cousin
MENGELE	8. Elie saw this notorious doctor
TZIPORA	9. The youngest of the Wiesel children
HILDA	10. The eldest of the Wiesel children
TIBI	11. Dreamed of going to Haifa with Elie and Yossi
GLEIWITZ	12. The marchers' destination
AMERICAN	13. An ___ tank was at the gates of Buchenwald
DYSENTERY	14. Mr. Wiesel had this ailment when he died
RUSSIANS	15. They liberated the men in the hospital
GHETTOS	16. Two ___ were set up in Sighet
AUSCHWITZ	17. Had a sign that said "Work is liberty!"
PASSOVER	18. The Germans arrested the Jewish leaders on the seventh day of ___
MARTHA	19. Offered the family safe refuge in her village
FASCISTS	20. They attacked Jewish shops and synagogues

Night Fill In The Blank 2

_____

_____

_____

_____

_____

_____

_____

_____

_____

_____

_____

_____

_____

_____

_____

_____

_____

_____

_____

_____

1. One Jew said he was the only one who had kept his promises
2. Told Elie he had not been written down
3. Akiba ____ thought God was testing the Jews
4. Mr. Wiesel didn't recognize this cousin
5. Jews had to wear the yellow ____
6. The only son
7. He tried to warn the Jews in Sighet: ____ the Beadle
8. The Jewish New Year: ____ Hashanah
9. Jewish musicians were not allowed to play this composer's music
10. The German security police
11. The reception center for Auschwitz
12. It ____ during the entire evacuation march
13. Elie saw this notorious doctor
14. Woman who had a vision of the furnaces
15. The German Jew who headed the block at Buna
16. Elie had surgery on his ____
17. Elie's father's first name
18. The Rabbi ____ was looking for his son
19. This idea began to fascinate Elie during the evacuation
20. The men had to ____ the block before they evacuated

Night Fill In The Blank 2 Answer Key

HITLER	1. One Jew said he was the only one who had kept his promises
YOSSI	2. Told Elie he had not been written down
DRUMER	3. Akiba ___ thought God was testing the Jews
STEIN	4. Mr. Wiesel didn't recognize this cousin
STAR	5. Jews had to wear the yellow ___
ELIE	6. The only son
MOSHE	7. He tried to warn the Jews in Sighet: ___ the Beadle
ROSH	8. The Jewish New Year: ___ Hashanah
BEETHOVEN	9. Jewish musicians were not allowed to play this composer's music
GESTAPO	10. The German security police
BIRKENAU	11. The reception center for Auschwitz
SNOWED	12. It ___ during the entire evacuation march
MENGELE	13. Elie saw this notorious doctor
SCHACHTER	14. Woman who had a vision of the furnaces
ALPHONSE	15. The German Jew who headed the block at Buna
FOOT	16. Elie had surgery on his ___
CHLOMO	17. Elie's father's first name
ELIAHOU	18. The Rabbi ___ was looking for his son
DYING	19. This idea began to fascinate Elie during the evacuation
CLEAN	20. The men had to ___ the block before they evacuated

Night Fill In The Blank 3

_____
_____
_____
_____
_____
_____
_____
_____
_____
_____
_____
_____
_____
_____
_____
_____
_____
_____
_____
_____

1. The men recited this prayer for themselves
2. Told Elie he had not been written down
3. It was crushed along with Juliek
4. Two ___ were set up in Sighet
5. Mr. Wiesel had this ailment when he died
6. Dreamed of going to Haifa with Elie and Yossi
7. It ___ during the entire evacuation march
8. Had a sign that said "Work is liberty!"
9. Elie's father's first name
10. This idea began to fascinate Elie during the evacuation
11. The next eldest of the Wiesel children
12. Akiba ___ thought God was testing the Jews
13. A tradesman turned policeman
14. He tried to warn the Jews in Sighet: ___ the Beadle
15. Elie Wiesel grew up in this town
16. The youngest of the Wiesel children
17. The Jewish New Year: ___ Hashanah
18. The German Jew who headed the block at Buna
19. It was the gravest danger
20. The German security police

Night Fill In The Blank 3 Answer Key

KADDISH	1. The men recited this prayer for themselves
YOSSI	2. Told Elie he had not been written down
VIOLIN	3. It was crushed along with Juliek
GHETTOS	4. Two ___ were set up in Sighet
DYSENTERY	5. Mr. Wiesel had this ailment when he died
TIBI	6. Dreamed of going to Haifa with Elie and Yossi
SNOWED	7. It ___ during the entire evacuation march
AUSCHWITZ	8. Had a sign that said "Work is liberty!"
CHLOMO	9. Elie's father's first name
DYING	10. This idea began to fascinate Elie during the evacuation
BEA	11. The next eldest of the Wiesel children
DRUMER	12. Akiba ___ thought God was testing the Jews
STERN	13. A tradesman turned policeman
MOSHE	14. He tried to warn the Jews in Sighet: ___ the Beadle
SIGHET	15. Elie Wiesel grew up in this town
TZIPORA	16. The youngest of the Wiesel children
ROSH	17. The Jewish New Year: ___ Hashanah
ALPHONSE	18. The German Jew who headed the block at Buna
SELECTION	19. It was the gravest danger
GESTAPO	20. The German security police

Night Fill In The Blank 4

_____

_____

_____

_____

_____

_____

_____

_____

_____

_____

_____

_____

_____

_____

_____

_____

_____

_____

_____

_____

1. Elie Wiesel grew up in this town
2. The reception center for Auschwitz
3. Elie's inheritance was a knife and a ___
4. The men had to ___ the block before they evacuated
5. This movement rescued the prisoners at Buchenwald
6. The marchers' destination
7. Elie saw this notorious doctor
8. Two ___ were set up in Sighet
9. It was the gravest danger
10. It once tasted like corpses
11. Elie hated these police first
12. Dreamed of going to Haifa with Elie and Yossi
13. It ___ during the entire evacuation march
14. Elie did not do this on Yom Kippur
15. Mr. Wiesel had this ailment when he died
16. Mr. Wiesel died in this camp
17. Elie and his father did not stay here, but joined the evacuation
18. The Jewish New Year: ___ Hashanah
19. Meir ___ died in the wagon
20. Elie had surgery on his ___

Night Fill In The Blank 4 Answer Key

SIGHET	1. Elie Wiesel grew up in this town
BIRKENAU	2. The reception center for Auschwitz
SPOON	3. Elie's inheritance was a knife and a ___
CLEAN	4. The men had to ___ the block before they evacuated
RESISTANCE	5. This movement rescued the prisoners at Buchenwald
GLEIWITZ	6. The marchers' destination
MENGELE	7. Elie saw this notorious doctor
GHETTOS	8. Two ___ were set up in Sighet
SELECTION	9. It was the gravest danger
SOUP	10. It once tasted like corpses
HUNGARIAN	11. Elie hated these police first
TIBI	12. Dreamed of going to Haifa with Elie and Yossi
SNOWED	13. It ___ during the entire evacuation march
FAST	14. Elie did not do this on Yom Kippur
DYSENTERY	15. Mr. Wiesel had this ailment when he died
BUCHENWALD	16. Mr. Wiesel died in this camp
HOSPITAL	17. Elie and his father did not stay here, but joined the evacuation
ROSH	18. The Jewish New Year: ___ Hashanah
KATZ	19. Meir ___ died in the wagon
FOOT	20. Elie had surgery on his ___

Night Matching 1

___ 1. MARTHA   A. A tradesman turned policeman
___ 2. CLEAN   B. The Germans arrested the Jewish leaders on the seventh day of ___
___ 3. BIRKENAU   C. This movement rescued the prisoners at Buchenwald
___ 4. BEA   D. The next eldest of the Wiesel children
___ 5. TRANSYLVANIA   E. Had a sign that said "Work is liberty!"
___ 6. PASSOVER   F. The country where Elie Wiesel grew up
___ 7. ROSH   G. The Kapo who had bouts of madness
___ 8. DRUMER   H. The only son
___ 9. ELIAHOU   I. Elie wanted his family to move here
___10. YOSSI   J. Offered the family safe refuge in her village
___11. SCHACHTER   K. Elie Wiesel grew up in this town
___12. IDEK   L. The Jewish New Year: ___ Hashanah
___13. SIGHET   M. Meir ___ died in the wagon
___14. RUSSIANS   N. Elie and his father did not stay here, but joined the evacuation
___15. PALESTINE   O. Told Elie he had not been written down
___16. RESISTANCE   P. Akiba ___ thought God was testing the Jews
___17. HOSPITAL   Q. Elie hated these police first
___18. KATZ   R. They liberated the men in the hospital
___19. STEIN   S. It ___ during the entire evacuation march
___20. STERN   T. Woman who had a vision of the furnaces
___21. HUNGARIAN   U. Mr. Wiesel didn't recognize this cousin
___22. ELIE   V. The Rabbi ___ was looking for his son
___23. SNOWED   W. It was the gravest danger
___24. SELECTION   X. The reception center for Auschwitz
___25. AUSCHWITZ   Y. The men had to ___ the block before they evacuated

Night Matching 1 Answer Key

J - 1. MARTHA	A.	A tradesman turned policeman
Y - 2. CLEAN	B.	The Germans arrested the Jewish leaders on the seventh day of ___
X - 3. BIRKENAU	C.	This movement rescued the prisoners at Buchenwald
D - 4. BEA	D.	The next eldest of the Wiesel children
F - 5. TRANSYLVANIA	E.	Had a sign that said "Work is liberty!"
B - 6. PASSOVER	F.	The country where Elie Wiesel grew up
L - 7. ROSH	G.	The Kapo who had bouts of madness
P - 8. DRUMER	H.	The only son
V - 9. ELIAHOU	I.	Elie wanted his family to move here
O -10. YOSSI	J.	Offered the family safe refuge in her village
T -11. SCHACHTER	K.	Elie Wiesel grew up in this town
G -12. IDEK	L.	The Jewish New Year: ___ Hashanah
K -13. SIGHET	M.	Meir ___ died in the wagon
R -14. RUSSIANS	N.	Elie and his father did not stay here, but joined the evacuation
I - 15. PALESTINE	O.	Told Elie he had not been written down
C -16. RESISTANCE	P.	Akiba ___ thought God was testing the Jews
N -17. HOSPITAL	Q.	Elie hated these police first
M -18. KATZ	R.	They liberated the men in the hospital
U -19. STEIN	S.	It ___ during the entire evacuation march
A -20. STERN	T.	Woman who had a vision of the furnaces
Q -21. HUNGARIAN	U.	Mr. Wiesel didn't recognize this cousin
H -22. ELIE	V.	The Rabbi ___ was looking for his son
S -23. SNOWED	W.	It was the gravest danger
W -24. SELECTION	X.	The reception center for Auschwitz
E -25. AUSCHWITZ	Y.	The men had to ___ the block before they evacuated

Night Matching 2

___ 1. HILDA
___ 2. HOSPITAL
___ 3. YOSSI
___ 4. ELIE
___ 5. STEIN
___ 6. RESISTANCE
___ 7. JULIEK
___ 8. KIPPUR
___ 9. PALESTINE
___ 10. RUSSIANS
___ 11. SPOON
___ 12. IDEK
___ 13. ALPHONSE
___ 14. GESTAPO
___ 15. TZIPORA
___ 16. ROSH
___ 17. BEA
___ 18. AMERICAN
___ 19. FAST
___ 20. BUNA
___ 21. MENGELE
___ 22. SOUP
___ 23. SELECTION
___ 24. BIRKENAU
___ 25. MOSHE

A. He tried to warn the Jews in Sighet: ___ the Beadle
B. The only son
C. The eldest of the Wiesel children
D. An ___ tank was at the gates of Buchenwald
E. Told Elie he had not been written down
F. Played his violin for the dying men
G. Elie's inheritance was a knife and a ___
H. Elie saw this notorious doctor
I. The youngest of the Wiesel children
J. Elie did not do this on Yom Kippur
K. The Day of Atonement: Yom ___
L. The next eldest of the Wiesel children
M. It was the gravest danger
N. Mr. Wiesel didn't recognize this cousin
O. The reception center for Auschwitz
P. Elie and his father did not stay here, but joined the evacuation
Q. It once tasted like corpses
R. This movement rescued the prisoners at Buchenwald
S. The Kapo who had bouts of madness
T. Elie wanted his family to move here
U. The Jewish New Year: ___ Hashanah
V. The German Jew who headed the block at Buna
W. They walked here from Auschwitz
X. The German security police
Y. They liberated the men in the hospital

Night Matching 2 Answer Key

C - 1. HILDA	A. He tried to warn the Jews in Sighet: ___ the Beadle
P - 2. HOSPITAL	B. The only son
E - 3. YOSSI	C. The eldest of the Wiesel children
B - 4. ELIE	D. An ___ tank was at the gates of Buchenwald
N - 5. STEIN	E. Told Elie he had not been written down
R - 6. RESISTANCE	F. Played his violin for the dying men
F - 7. JULIEK	G. Elie's inheritance was a knife and a ___
K - 8. KIPPUR	H. Elie saw this notorious doctor
T - 9. PALESTINE	I. The youngest of the Wiesel children
Y - 10. RUSSIANS	J. Elie did not do this on Yom Kippur
G - 11. SPOON	K. The Day of Atonement: Yom ___
S - 12. IDEK	L. The next eldest of the Wiesel children
V - 13. ALPHONSE	M. It was the gravest danger
X - 14. GESTAPO	N. Mr. Wiesel didn't recognize this cousin
I - 15. TZIPORA	O. The reception center for Auschwitz
U - 16. ROSH	P. Elie and his father did not stay here, but joined the evacuation
L - 17. BEA	Q. It once tasted like corpses
D - 18. AMERICAN	R. This movement rescued the prisoners at Buchenwald
J - 19. FAST	S. The Kapo who had bouts of madness
W - 20. BUNA	T. Elie wanted his family to move here
H - 21. MENGELE	U. The Jewish New Year: ___ Hashanah
Q - 22. SOUP	V. The German Jew who headed the block at Buna
M - 23. SELECTION	W. They walked here from Auschwitz
O - 24. BIRKENAU	X. The German security police
A - 25. MOSHE	Y. They liberated the men in the hospital

Copyrighted

Night Matching 3

___ 1. RUSSIANS   A. An ___ tank was at the gates of Buchenwald
___ 2. BEETHOVEN   B. The eldest of the Wiesel children
___ 3. MARTHA   C. Akiba ___ thought God was testing the Jews
___ 4. CLEAN   D. Elie did not do this on Yom Kippur
___ 5. GHETTOS   E. Jewish musicians were not allowed to play this composer's music
___ 6. AUSCHWITZ   F. He tormented Elie's father to get Elie's gold tooth
___ 7. DYSENTERY   G. A tradesman turned policeman
___ 8. DRUMER   H. Played his violin for the dying men
___ 9. HUNGARIAN   I. The marchers' destination
___10. KADDISH   J. The Day of Atonement: Yom ___
___11. FOOT   K. The men had to ___ the block before they evacuated
___12. GLEIWITZ   L. The prisoners ate this and soup
___13. HILDA   M. The men recited this prayer for themselves
___14. DYING   N. Offered the family safe refuge in her village
___15. AMERICAN   O. Woman who had a vision of the furnaces
___16. KIPPUR   P. They liberated the men in the hospital
___17. BREAD   Q. Two ___ were set up in Sighet
___18. JULIEK   R. Had a sign that said "Work is liberty!"
___19. SCHACHTER   S. Elie hated these police first
___20. FAST   T. They walked here from Auschwitz
___21. PASSOVER   U. This idea began to fascinate Elie during the evacuation
___22. FRANEK   V. Told Elie he had not been written down
___23. BUNA   W. Elie had surgery on his ___
___24. STERN   X. Mr. Wiesel had this ailment when he died
___25. YOSSI   Y. The Germans arrested the Jewish leaders on the seventh day of ___

Night Matching 3 Answer Key

P - 1. RUSSIANS	A.	An ___ tank was at the gates of Buchenwald
E - 2. BEETHOVEN	B.	The eldest of the Wiesel children
N - 3. MARTHA	C.	Akiba ___ thought God was testing the Jews
K - 4. CLEAN	D.	Elie did not do this on Yom Kippur
Q - 5. GHETTOS	E.	Jewish musicians were not allowed to play this composer's music
R - 6. AUSCHWITZ	F.	He tormented Elie's father to get Elie's gold tooth
X - 7. DYSENTERY	G.	A tradesman turned policeman
C - 8. DRUMER	H.	Played his violin for the dying men
S - 9. HUNGARIAN	I.	The marchers' destination
M -10. KADDISH	J.	The Day of Atonement: Yom ___
W -11. FOOT	K.	The men had to ___ the block before they evacuated
I - 12. GLEIWITZ	L.	The prisoners ate this and soup
B -13. HILDA	M.	The men recited this prayer for themselves
U -14. DYING	N.	Offered the family safe refuge in her village
A -15. AMERICAN	O.	Woman who had a vision of the furnaces
J - 16. KIPPUR	P.	They liberated the men in the hospital
L - 17. BREAD	Q.	Two ___ were set up in Sighet
H -18. JULIEK	R.	Had a sign that said "Work is liberty!"
O -19. SCHACHTER	S.	Elie hated these police first
D -20. FAST	T.	They walked here from Auschwitz
Y -21. PASSOVER	U.	This idea began to fascinate Elie during the evacuation
F -22. FRANEK	V.	Told Elie he had not been written down
T -23. BUNA	W.	Elie had surgery on his ___
G -24. STERN	X.	Mr. Wiesel had this ailment when he died
V -25. YOSSI	Y.	The Germans arrested the Jewish leaders on the seventh day of ___

Night Matching 4

___ 1. VIOLIN   A. Mr. Wiesel didn't recognize this cousin
___ 2. BIRKENAU   B. The country where Elie Wiesel grew up
___ 3. TRANSYLVANIA   C. It was crushed along with Juliek
___ 4. STAR   D. It was the gravest danger
___ 5. STEIN   E. The next eldest of the Wiesel children
___ 6. BEA   F. It once tasted like corpses
___ 7. HUNGARIAN   G. The Day of Atonement: Yom ___
___ 8. GESTAPO   H. The marchers' destination
___ 9. MARTHA   I. Elie Wiesel grew up in this town
___10. DYSENTERY   J. Jews had to wear the yellow ___
___11. CHLOMO   K. Elie did not do this on Yom Kippur
___12. STERN   L. The German security police
___13. SNOWED   M. Mr. Wiesel had this ailment when he died
___14. KATZ   N. An ___ tank was at the gates of Buchenwald
___15. SIGHET   O. Offered the family safe refuge in her village
___16. KADDISH   P. It ___ during the entire evacuation march
___17. KIPPUR   Q. A Polish boy who was trampled during the evacuation
___18. SPOON   R. He tried to warn the Jews in Sighet: ___ the Beadle
___19. GLEIWITZ   S. Elie's father's first name
___20. MOSHE   T. Elie hated these police first
___21. SELECTION   U. Elie's inheritance was a knife and a ___
___22. AMERICAN   V. The reception center for Auschwitz
___23. FAST   W. The men recited this prayer for themselves
___24. SOUP   X. A tradesman turned policeman
___25. ZALMAN   Y. Meir ___ died in the wagon

Night Matching 4 Answer Key

C - 1. VIOLIN	A.	Mr. Wiesel didn't recognize this cousin
V - 2. BIRKENAU	B.	The country where Elie Wiesel grew up
B - 3. TRANSYLVANIA	C.	It was crushed along with Juliek
J - 4. STAR	D.	It was the gravest danger
A - 5. STEIN	E.	The next eldest of the Wiesel children
E - 6. BEA	F.	It once tasted like corpses
T - 7. HUNGARIAN	G.	The Day of Atonement: Yom ___
L - 8. GESTAPO	H.	The marchers' destination
O - 9. MARTHA	I.	Elie Wiesel grew up in this town
M -10. DYSENTERY	J.	Jews had to wear the yellow ___
S -11. CHLOMO	K.	Elie did not do this on Yom Kippur
X -12. STERN	L.	The German security police
P -13. SNOWED	M.	Mr. Wiesel had this ailment when he died
Y -14. KATZ	N.	An ___ tank was at the gates of Buchenwald
I - 15. SIGHET	O.	Offered the family safe refuge in her village
W -16. KADDISH	P.	It ___ during the entire evacuation march
G -17. KIPPUR	Q.	A Polish boy who was trampled during the evacuation
U -18. SPOON	R.	He tried to warn the Jews in Sighet: ___ the Beadle
H -19. GLEIWITZ	S.	Elie's father's first name
R -20. MOSHE	T.	Elie hated these police first
D -21. SELECTION	U.	Elie's inheritance was a knife and a ___
N -22. AMERICAN	V.	The reception center for Auschwitz
K -23. FAST	W.	The men recited this prayer for themselves
F -24. SOUP	X.	A tradesman turned policeman
Q -25. ZALMAN	Y.	Meir ___ died in the wagon

Night Magic Squares 1

A. SNOWED G. CHLOMO M. KIPPUR
B. STEIN H. ELIAHOU N. VIOLIN
C. JULIEK I. CLEAN O. GESTAPO
D. SCHACHTER J. BUCHENWALD P. RESISTANCE
E. BUNA K. FRANEK
F. MENGELE L. BIRKENAU

1. The German security police
2. Woman who had a vision of the furnaces
3. Mr. Wiesel died in this camp
4. They walked here from Auschwitz
5. The men had to ___ the block before they evacuated
6. Elie saw this notorious doctor
7. This movement rescued the prisoners at Buchenwald
8. Played his violin for the dying men
9. The Rabbi ___ was looking for his son
10. He tormented Elie's father to get Elie's gold tooth
11. It ___ during the entire evacuation march
12. It was crushed along with Juliek
13. Mr. Wiesel didn't recognize this cousin
14. The Day of Atonement: Yom ___
15. Elie's father's first name
16. The reception center for Auschwitz

A=	B=	C=	D=
E=	F=	G=	H=
I=	J=	K=	L=
M=	N=	O=	P=

Night Magic Squares 1 Answer Key

A. SNOWED
B. STEIN
C. JULIEK
D. SCHACHTER
E. BUNA
F. MENGELE
G. CHLOMO
H. ELIAHOU
I. CLEAN
J. BUCHENWALD
K. FRANEK
L. BIRKENAU
M. KIPPUR
N. VIOLIN
O. GESTAPO
P. RESISTANCE

1. The German security police
2. Woman who had a vision of the furnaces
3. Mr. Wiesel died in this camp
4. They walked here from Auschwitz
5. The men had to ___ the block before they evacuated
6. Elie saw this notorious doctor
7. This movement rescued the prisoners at Buchenwald
8. Played his violin for the dying men
9. The Rabbi ___ was looking for his son
10. He tormented Elie's father to get Elie's gold tooth
11. It ___ during the entire evacuation march
12. It was crushed along with Juliek
13. Mr. Wiesel didn't recognize this cousin
14. The Day of Atonement: Yom ___
15. Elie's father's first name
16. The reception center for Auschwitz

A=11	B=13	C=8	D=2
E=4	F=6	G=15	H=9
I=5	J=3	K=10	L=16
M=14	N=12	O=1	P=7

Night Magic Squares 2

A. SPOON
B. GESTAPO
C. TIBI
D. FRANEK
E. BUNA
F. DRUMER
G. FOOT
H. ALPHONSE
I. BUCHENWALD
J. YOSSI
K. STEIN
L. TRANSYLVANIA
M. SELECTION
N. SOUP
O. RUSSIANS
P. RESISTANCE

1. The German Jew who headed the block at Buna
2. It was the gravest danger
3. The German security police
4. Mr. Wiesel didn't recognize this cousin
5. Told Elie he had not been written down
6. Dreamed of going to Haifa with Elie and Yossi
7. This movement rescued the prisoners at Buchenwald
8. They walked here from Auschwitz
9. They liberated the men in the hospital
10. Akiba ___ thought God was testing the Jews
11. Mr. Wiesel died in this camp
12. He tormented Elie's father to get Elie's gold tooth
13. Elie's inheritance was a knife and a ___
14. The country where Elie Wiesel grew up
15. Elie had surgery on his ___
16. It once tasted like corpses

A=	B=	C=	D=
E=	F=	G=	H=
I=	J=	K=	L=
M=	N=	O=	P=

Night Magic Squares 2 Answer Key

A. SPOON
B. GESTAPO
C. TIBI
D. FRANEK
E. BUNA
F. DRUMER
G. FOOT
H. ALPHONSE
I. BUCHENWALD
J. YOSSI
K. STEIN
L. TRANSYLVANIA
M. SELECTION
N. SOUP
O. RUSSIANS
P. RESISTANCE

1. The German Jew who headed the block at Buna
2. It was the gravest danger
3. The German security police
4. Mr. Wiesel didn't recognize this cousin
5. Told Elie he had not been written down
6. Dreamed of going to Haifa with Elie and Yossi
7. This movement rescued the prisoners at Buchenwald
8. They walked here from Auschwitz
9. They liberated the men in the hospital
10. Akiba ___ thought God was testing the Jews
11. Mr. Wiesel died in this camp
12. He tormented Elie's father to get Elie's gold tooth
13. Elie's inheritance was a knife and a ___
14. The country where Elie Wiesel grew up
15. Elie had surgery on his ___
16. It once tasted like corpses

A=13	B=3	C=6	D=12
E=8	F=10	G=15	H=1
I=11	J=5	K=4	L=14
M=2	N=16	O=9	P=7

Night Magic Squares 3

A. SCHACHTER
B. KATZ
C. BUCHENWALD
D. BIRKENAU
E. MARTHA
F. SOUP
G. IDEK
H. GESTAPO
I. PALESTINE
J. MENGELE
K. ZALMAN
L. RUSSIANS
M. YOSSI
N. RESISTANCE
O. BUNA
P. HUNGARIAN

1. They walked here from Auschwitz
2. Elie saw this notorious doctor
3. The German security police
4. Woman who had a vision of the furnaces
5. The reception center for Auschwitz
6. Offered the family safe refuge in her village
7. A Polish boy who was trampled during the evacuation
8. This movement rescued the prisoners at Buchenwald
9. It once tasted like corpses
10. Mr. Wiesel died in this camp
11. Told Elie he had not been written down
12. They liberated the men in the hospital
13. Elie wanted his family to move here
14. Elie hated these police first
15. Meir ___ died in the wagon
16. The Kapo who had bouts of madness

A=	B=	C=	D=
E=	F=	G=	H=
I=	J=	K=	L=
M=	N=	O=	P=

Night Magic Squares 3 Answer Key

A. SCHACHTER
B. KATZ
C. BUCHENWALD
D. BIRKENAU
E. MARTHA
F. SOUP
G. IDEK
H. GESTAPO
I. PALESTINE
J. MENGELE
K. ZALMAN
L. RUSSIANS
M. YOSSI
N. RESISTANCE
O. BUNA
P. HUNGARIAN

1. They walked here from Auschwitz
2. Elie saw this notorious doctor
3. The German security police
4. Woman who had a vision of the furnaces
5. The reception center for Auschwitz
6. Offered the family safe refuge in her village
7. A Polish boy who was trampled during the evacuation
8. This movement rescued the prisoners at Buchenwald
9. It once tasted like corpses
10. Mr. Wiesel died in this camp
11. Told Elie he had not been written down
12. They liberated the men in the hospital
13. Elie wanted his family to move here
14. Elie hated these police first
15. Meir ___ died in the wagon
16. The Kapo who had bouts of madness

A=4	B=15	C=10	D=5
E=6	F=9	G=16	H=3
I=13	J=2	K=7	L=12
M=11	N=8	O=1	P=14

Night Magic Squares 4

A. MARTHA
B. HOSPITAL
C. SCHACHTER
D. GESTAPO
E. HITLER
F. BIRKENAU
G. BUCHENWALD
H. BUNA
I. STEIN
J. KIPPUR
K. KATZ
L. BEETHOVEN
M. SOUP
N. RUSSIANS
O. PALESTINE
P. CLEAN

1. It once tasted like corpses
2. The reception center for Auschwitz
3. They walked here from Auschwitz
4. Elie wanted his family to move here
5. Jewish musicians were not allowed to play this composer's music
6. Woman who had a vision of the furnaces
7. Offered the family safe refuge in her village
8. The Day of Atonement: Yom ___
9. Meir ___ died in the wagon
10. The German security police
11. Elie and his father did not stay here, but joined the evacuation
12. Mr. Wiesel didn't recognize this cousin
13. They liberated the men in the hospital
14. One Jew said he was the only one who had kept his promises
15. Mr. Wiesel died in this camp
16. The men had to ___ the block before they evacuated

A=	B=	C=	D=
E=	F=	G=	H=
I=	J=	K=	L=
M=	N=	O=	P=

Night Magic Squares 4 Answer Key

A. MARTHA
B. HOSPITAL
C. SCHACHTER
D. GESTAPO
E. HITLER
F. BIRKENAU
G. BUCHENWALD
H. BUNA
I. STEIN
J. KIPPUR
K. KATZ
L. BEETHOVEN
M. SOUP
N. RUSSIANS
O. PALESTINE
P. CLEAN

1. It once tasted like corpses
2. The reception center for Auschwitz
3. They walked here from Auschwitz
4. Elie wanted his family to move here
5. Jewish musicians were not allowed to play this composer's music
6. Woman who had a vision of the furnaces
7. Offered the family safe refuge in her village
8. The Day of Atonement: Yom ___
9. Meir ___ died in the wagon
10. The German security police
11. Elie and his father did not stay here, but joined the evacuation
12. Mr. Wiesel didn't recognize this cousin
13. They liberated the men in the hospital
14. One Jew said he was the only one who had kept his promises
15. Mr. Wiesel died in this camp
16. The men had to ___ the block before they evacuated

A=7	B=11	C=6	D=10
E=14	F=2	G=15	H=3
I=12	J=8	K=9	L=5
M=1	N=13	O=4	P=16

Night Word Search 1

```
R O S H B E E T H O V E N C R B R K
T S J I Q G Z L W A N I L U S I E D
C Q E T S Z T Q N I L E P I N R S A
M Q L L T Z Q U T O A P K R E K I V
A P Z E E P B S I N I D E K A E S Y
R M R R I C E V T K B T I D Y N T J
T W E P N L T D P A S L T T A A P
H A M R A S Z I P Y R I U R Z U N M
A S U P I R O G O A H S J K M G C Y
G C R S P C L U R N S T P W A Y E B
P H D G C E A O P M S S I O Q T S T
F A S T I H P N S O I N O B O X Z F
G C L W D I W O W S G F O V I N Z V
N H I P Z Y T I S H H R W W E Z T J
H T F T H T O T E E A D A E R B G
Z E J O E O Y N H Z T N H P Z D J J
M R M H O F N Y G Z F E Z A L M A N
N N G W R T Q S R G K K A D D I S H
G E S T A P O B E R U S S I A N S M
```

A Polish boy who was trampled during the evacuation (6)
A tradesman turned policeman (5)
Akiba ___ thought God was testing the Jews (6)
An ___ tank was at the gates of Buchenwald (8)
Dreamed of going to Haifa with Elie and Yossi (4)
Elie Wiesel grew up in this town (6)
Elie did not do this on Yom Kippur (4)
Elie had surgery on his ___ (4)
Elie wanted his family to move here (9)
Elie's inheritance was a knife and a ___ (5)
Had a sign that said "Work is liberty!" (9)
He tormented Elie's father to get Elie's gold tooth (6)
He tried to warn the Jews in Sighet: ___ the Beadle (5)
It __ during the entire evacuation march (6)
It once tasted like corpses (4)
It was crushed along with Juliek (6)
It was the gravest danger (9)
Jewish musicians were not allowed to play this composer's music (9)
Jews had to wear the yellow ___ (4)
Meir ___ died in the wagon (4)
Mr. Wiesel didn't recognize this cousin (5)
Offered the family safe refuge in her village (6)
One Jew said he was the only one who had kept his promises (6)

Played his violin for the dying men (6)
The Day of Atonement: Yom ___ (6)
The German Jew who headed the block at Buna (8)
The German security police (7)
The Germans arrested the Jewish leaders on the seventh day of ___ (8)
The Jewish New Year: ___ Hashanah (4)
The Kapo who had bouts of madness (4)
The eldest of the Wiesel children (5)
The marchers' destination (8)
The men had to ___ the block before they evacuated (5)
The men recited this prayer for themselves (7)
The next eldest of the Wiesel children (3)
The only son (4)
The prisoners ate this and soup (5)
The reception center for Auschwitz (8)
The youngest of the Wiesel children (7)
They liberated the men in the hospital (8)
They walked here from Auschwitz (4)
This idea began to fascinate Elie during the evacuation (5)
This movement rescued the prisoners at Buchenwald (10)
Told Elie he had not been written down (5)
Two ___ were set up in Sighet (7)
Woman who had a vision of the furnaces (9)

Night Word Search 1 Answer Key

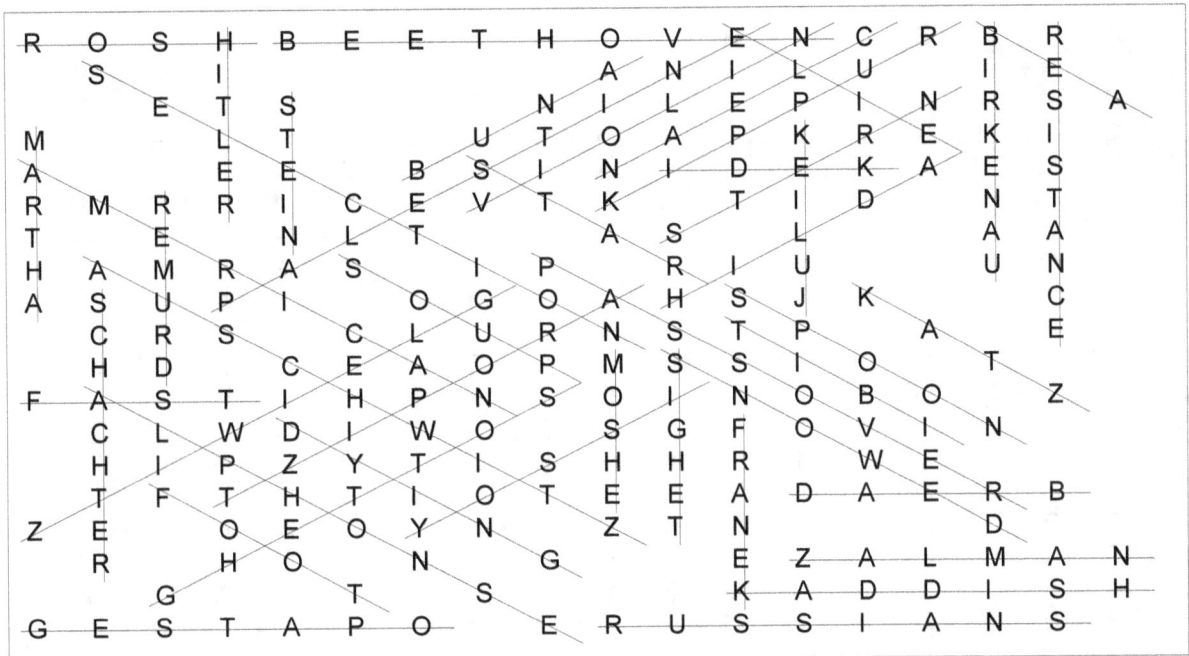

A Polish boy who was trampled during the evacuation (6)
A tradesman turned policeman (5)
Akiba ___ thought God was testing the Jews (6)
An ___ tank was at the gates of Buchenwald (8)
Dreamed of going to Haifa with Elie and Yossi (4)
Elie Wiesel grew up in this town (6)
Elie did not do this on Yom Kippur (4)
Elie had surgery on his ___ (4)
Elie wanted his family to move here (9)
Elie's inheritance was a knife and a ___ (5)
Had a sign that said "Work is liberty!" (9)
He tormented Elie's father to get Elie's gold tooth (6)
He tried to warn the Jews in Sighet: ___ the Beadle (5)
It ___ during the entire evacuation march (6)
It once tasted like corpses (4)
It was crushed along with Juliek (6)
It was the gravest danger (9)
Jewish musicians were not allowed to play this composer's music (9)
Jews had to wear the yellow ___ (4)
Meir ___ died in the wagon (4)
Mr. Wiesel didn't recognize this cousin (5)
Offered the family safe refuge in her village (6)
One Jew said he was the only one who had kept his promises (6)

Played his violin for the dying men (6)
The Day of Atonement: Yom ___ (6)
The German Jew who headed the block at Buna (8)
The German security police (7)
The Germans arrested the Jewish leaders on the seventh day of ___ (8)
The Jewish New Year: ___ Hashanah (4)
The Kapo who had bouts of madness (4)
The eldest of the Wiesel children (5)
The marchers' destination (8)
The men had to ___ the block before they evacuated (5)
The men recited this prayer for themselves (7)
The next eldest of the Wiesel children (3)
The only son (4)
The prisoners ate this and soup (5)
The reception center for Auschwitz (8)
The youngest of the Wiesel children (7)
They liberated the men in the hospital (8)
They walked here from Auschwitz (4)
This idea began to fascinate Elie during the evacuation (5)
This movement rescued the prisoners at Buchenwald (10)
Told Elie he had not been written down (5)
Two ___ were set up in Sighet (7)
Woman who had a vision of the furnaces (9)

Night Word Search 2

```
F A S T S V F H O S P I T A L G T D
O X R P T I S G U K N R T D Y E Z W
O X O A A O G P A N A O N T B S I G
T O N H R L S H N H G D W Y M T P K
N I E T S I E B E A E D E X A O J
A E S R B N L N K T L D R I D P R M
U C N A U J E H R L I L C I S O A V
S N O M C S C T I V E I T E A H C F
C A H J H F T K B T Z H G L C N Y H
H T P U E D I E W K L K N I R G T N
W S L L N N O S R E I E M A N N B X
I I A I W C N M N T P R H A I K D
T S D E A C L I M W F M P O C Y A S
Z E B K L I T E Y R F G Y U I D T K
B R E A D S N P A S S O V E R B Z L
F S R E E G I N X N K Y L U E U M F
R O K L E B E L C H L O M O M N K W
Z U A L I K Y O S S I E S P A A T B
Q P E T Z A L M A N R M O S H E K L
```

A Polish boy who was trampled during the evacuation (6)
A tradesman turned policeman (5)
Akiba ___ thought God was testing the Jews (6)
An ___ tank was at the gates of Buchenwald (8)
Dreamed of going to Haifa with Elie and Yossi (4)
Elie Wiesel grew up in this town (6)
Elie and his father did not stay here, but joined the evacuation (8)
Elie did not do this on Yom Kippur (4)
Elie had surgery on his ___ (4)
Elie hated these police first (9)
Elie saw this notorious doctor (7)
Elie wanted his family to move here (9)
Elie's father's first name (6)
Elie's inheritance was a knife and a ___ (5)
Had a sign that said "Work is liberty!" (9)
He tormented Elie's father to get Elie's gold tooth (6)
He tried to warn the Jews in Sighet: ___ the Beadle (5)
It __ during the entire evacuation march (6)
It once tasted like corpses (4)
It was crushed along with Juliek (6)
It was the gravest danger (9)
Jews had to wear the yellow ___ (4)
Meir ___ died in the wagon (4)
Mr. Wiesel didn't recognize this cousin (5)

Mr. Wiesel died in this camp (10)
Offered the family safe refuge in her village (6)
One Jew said he was the only one who had kept his promises (6)
Played his violin for the dying men (6)
The Day of Atonement: Yom ___ (6)
The German Jew who headed the block at Buna (8)
The German security police (7)
The Germans arrested the Jewish leaders on the seventh day of ___ (8)
The Jewish New Year: ___ Hashanah (4)
The Kapo who had bouts of madness (4)
The Rabbi ___ was looking for his son (7)
The eldest of the Wiesel children (5)
The men had to ___ the block before they evacuated (5)
The men recited this prayer for themselves (7)
The next eldest of the Wiesel children (3)
The only son (4)
The prisoners ate this and soup (5)
The reception center for Auschwitz (8)
The youngest of the Wiesel children (7)
They walked here from Auschwitz (4)
This idea began to fascinate Elie during the evacuation (5)
This movement rescued the prisoners at Buchenwald (10)
Told Elie he had not been written down (5)

Night Word Search 2 Answer Key

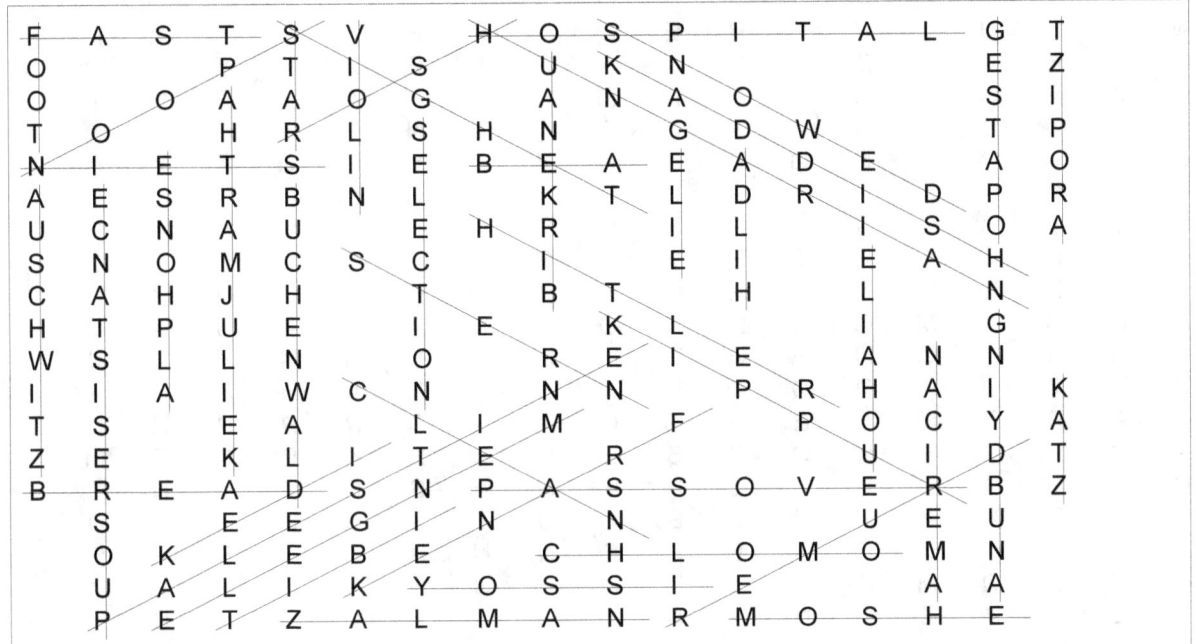

A Polish boy who was trampled during the evacuation (6)
A tradesman turned policeman (5)
Akiba ___ thought God was testing the Jews (6)
An ___ tank was at the gates of Buchenwald (8)
Dreamed of going to Haifa with Elie and Yossi (4)
Elie Wiesel grew up in this town (6)
Elie and his father did not stay here, but joined the evacuation (8)
Elie did not do this on Yom Kippur (4)
Elie had surgery on his ___ (4)
Elie hated these police first (9)
Elie saw this notorious doctor (7)
Elie wanted his family to move here (9)
Elie's father's first name (6)
Elie's inheritance was a knife and a ___ (5)
Had a sign that said "Work is liberty!" (9)
He tormented Elie's father to get Elie's gold tooth (6)
He tried to warn the Jews in Sighet: ___ the Beadle (5)
It __ during the entire evacuation march (6)
It once tasted like corpses (4)
It was crushed along with Juliek (6)
It was the gravest danger (9)
Jews had to wear the yellow ___ (4)
Meir ___ died in the wagon (4)
Mr. Wiesel didn't recognize this cousin (5)

Mr. Wiesel died in this camp (10)
Offered the family safe refuge in her village (6)
One Jew said he was the only one who had kept his promises (6)
Played his violin for the dying men (6)
The Day of Atonement: Yom ___ (6)
The German Jew who headed the block at Buna (8)
The German security police (7)
The Germans arrested the Jewish leaders on the seventh day of ___ (8)
The Jewish New Year: ___ Hashanah (4)
The Kapo who had bouts of madness (4)
The Rabbi ___ was looking for his son (7)
The eldest of the Wiesel children (5)
The men had to ___ the block before they evacuated (5)
The men recited this prayer for themselves (7)
The next eldest of the Wiesel children (3)
The only son (4)
The prisoners ate this and soup (5)
The reception center for Auschwitz (8)
The youngest of the Wiesel children (7)
They walked here from Auschwitz (4)
This idea began to fascinate Elie during the evacuation (5)
This movement rescued the prisoners at Buchenwald (10)
Told Elie he had not been written down (5)

Night Word Search 3

```
N I L O I V E R E L T I H K P T Y L
O X F S A Z L M A N Z E P R Y M D
I X S O M R R G I M C I N P T F N T
T Y N U E D L F P E L H Y P T P S Q
C B W P R E G V R U V S C O A Y D
E D C G I H N B J U Y R O F R Y T
L Y W C S K R M L S M S L V E A Q
E R I I A E T E V T G S A C Z B C
S T E I N P A L E S T I A N E U N
Z K C A M G N D R O I D A A U A N
C H R Z G I W T B E T L N N S L G
T F T D A D Q T I K S L E A H S P N
M A R T H A E U G I M C R P P H S
K D X R M H O G S E R O E K B O L
D L M B G H Z E I S M S Y R J O M
B I Z X A F R Y B Z U T Y H O N D
W H D I V O S T E R N A X E S D
C H L O M O K A D I S H P F G S Y
P E Y R E T N E S Y D D E W O N F
```

ALPHONSE	ELIAHOU	JULIEK	SOUP
AMERICAN	ELIE	KADDISH	SPOON
BEA	FAST	KATZ	STAR
BIRKENAU	FOOT	MARTHA	STEIN
BREAD	FRANEK	MOSHE	STERN
BUNA	GESTAPO	PALESTINE	TIBI
CHLOMO	GHETTOS	RESISTANCE	TRANSYLVANIA
CLEAN	GLEIWITZ	ROSH	TZIPORA
DRUMER	HILDA	RUSSIANS	VIOLIN
DYING	HITLER	SELECTION	YOSSI
DYSENTERY	IDEK	SNOWED	ZALMAN

Night Word Search 3 Answer Key

```
N   I   L   O   I   V   E   R   E   L   T   I   H   K       T
O       S       A   Z   A   L   M   A   N   Z   E       R
I       O       M           G       E       I       A           T
T       U       E       L       R       L       N   P   C       S
C       P       R       B   J   U   Y       S   Y   O       O   A
E   D           I       R       L       S       S   L       F   R
L       Y   W   C   S   K       V       S       S   E       R   E
E       I   I   A   E   T       P   A   L   E   S   T   I   N   E   U   B
S       T   E   A       G   N   D   R   O   I   D   A       N       A   L
Z           I       N   I       T   B   E   T       N       N       P
        R   Z       A       T   I   K   S       E   A       S       H
M   A   R   T   H   A   E   U   G   I   M   K       R       P       O
K       D           H   O   S   E   R   O   E           P       N
    L               G       H       E       I   S   M   R       O       S
    I               A       F       R       B   U       H       O       E
    H                   I   O       S   T   E   R   N       T       E   H
C   H   L   O   M   O   K   A   D   D   I   S   H       P               S
    E   Y   R   E   T   N   E   S   Y   D   D   E   W   O   N   S
```

ALPHONSE	ELIAHOU	JULIEK	SOUP
AMERICAN	ELIE	KADDISH	SPOON
BEA	FAST	KATZ	STAR
BIRKENAU	FOOT	MARTHA	STEIN
BREAD	FRANEK	MOSHE	STERN
BUNA	GESTAPO	PALESTINE	TIBI
CHLOMO	GHETTOS	RESISTANCE	TRANSYLVANIA
CLEAN	GLEIWITZ	ROSH	TZIPORA
DRUMER	HILDA	RUSSIANS	VIOLIN
DYING	HITLER	SELECTION	YOSSI
DYSENTERY	IDEK	SNOWED	ZALMAN

Night Word Search 4

```
H O S P I T A L K T B A S B U N A W
R X U A D F H A T Z E U N C A E X Z
E O R L E Z T M R I E S O M C B V M
S Z G E K Z R P A P C W M E I X Z Y
I A K S B F A N S O H E O F R N M C
S L A T R S M Y S R W D S O G G B
T M D I E R W E A V I O E T M K Y B
A A N A D I V L S E T P D A L R T
N N I E D L Y Y V Z N Z E F E O I
C C S S E S Z I A P W Z T G A A S V
E F H I T L E R N O O P S N F T H T
G A K L J A F W I G E F E M H S G S
V S I S O P R X A S B S G Y O D H Z
J C P T L M N X N Y V I S Y D R E N
U I P J M S O O S V X G Q L I U T T
L S U C U O H A I L E H Y B D M T N
I T R P M P H I L D A E I D T E O D
E S Y V L G L E I W I T Z M S R O S
K E N A R F S T E R N I L O I V S Y
```

ALPHONSE   ELIE   JULIEK   SOUP
AMERICAN   FASCISTS   KADDISH   SPOON
AUSCHWITZ   FAST   KATZ   STAR
BEA   FOOT   KIPPUR   STEIN
BEETHOVEN   FRANEK   MARTHA   STERN
BREAD   GESTAPO   MENGELE   TIBI
BUNA   GHETTOS   MOSHE   TRANSYLVANIA
CHLOMO   GLEIWITZ   PALESTINE   TZIPORA
CLEAN   HILDA   RESISTANCE   VIOLIN
DRUMER   HITLER   ROSH   YOSSI
DYING   HOSPITAL   SIGHET   ZALMAN
ELIAHOU   IDEK   SNOWED

Night Word Search 4 Answer Key

ALPHONSE	ELIE	JULIEK	SOUP
AMERICAN	FASCISTS	KADDISH	SPOON
AUSCHWITZ	FAST	KATZ	STAR
BEA	FOOT	KIPPUR	STEIN
BEETHOVEN	FRANEK	MARTHA	STERN
BREAD	GESTAPO	MENGELE	TIBI
BUNA	GHETTOS	MOSHE	TRANSYLVANIA
CHLOMO	GLEIWITZ	PALESTINE	TZIPORA
CLEAN	HILDA	RESISTANCE	VIOLIN
DRUMER	HITLER	ROSH	YOSSI
DYING	HOSPITAL	SIGHET	ZALMAN
ELIAHOU	IDEK	SNOWED	

Night Crossword 1

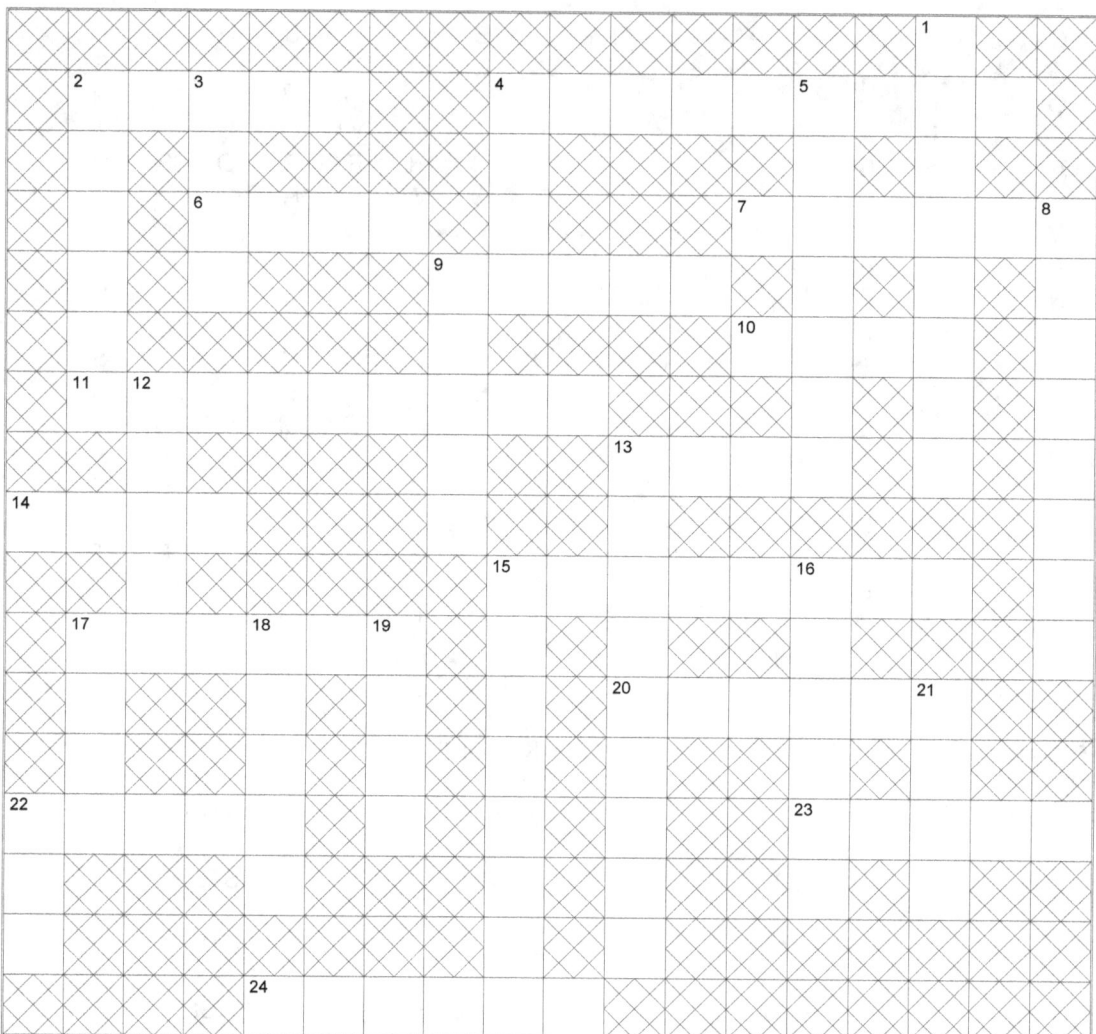

Across

2. A tradesman turned policeman
4. It was the gravest danger
6. The Kapo who had bouts of madness
7. The Day of Atonement: Yom ___
9. Elie's inheritance was a knife and a ___
10. Elie had surgery on his ___
11. Mr. Wiesel had this ailment when he died
13. They walked here from Auschwitz
14. Elie did not do this on Yom Kippur
15. An ___ tank was at the gates of Buchenwald
17. Elie Wiesel grew up in this town
20. One Jew said he was the only one who had kept his promises
22. The prisoners ate this and soup
23. He tried to warn the Jews in Sighet: ___ the Beadle
24. Played his violin for the dying men

Down

1. Elie and his father did not stay here, but joined the evacuation
2. It ___ during the entire evacuation march
3. The only son
4. It once tasted like corpses
5. The youngest of the Wiesel children
8. They liberated the men in the hospital
9. Mr. Wiesel didn't recognize this cousin
12. Told Elie he had not been written down
13. Jewish musicians were not allowed to play this composer's music
15. The German Jew who headed the block at Buna
16. Elie's father's first name
17. Jews had to wear the yellow ___
18. The eldest of the Wiesel children
19. Dreamed of going to Haifa with Elie and Yossi
21. The Jewish New Year: ___ Hashanah
22. The next eldest of the Wiesel children

Night Crossword 1 Answer Key

													¹H		
	²S	³T	E	R	N		⁴S	E	L	E	C	⁵T	I	O	N
	N		L				O					Z		S	
	O		⁶I	D	E	K		U			⁷K	I	P	P	U	⁸R
	W		E				⁹S	P	O	O	N		P		I		U
	E						T					¹⁰F	O	O	T		S
	¹¹D	¹²Y	S	E	N	T	E	R	Y			R		A		S
		O					I		¹³B	U	N	A		L		I
¹⁴F	A	S	T			N		E			¹⁶C	A	N		A
		S			¹⁵A	M	E	R	I	C	A	N				N
	¹⁷S	I	¹⁸G	H	¹⁹E	T		L		T		H				S
	T		I		I		L		²⁰H	I	T	L	E	²¹R	
	A		L		B		H		O		O		O	
²²B	R	E	A	D		I		O		V		²³M	O	S	H	E
E				A				N		E		O		H	
A								S		N					
			²⁴J	U	L	I	E	K							

Across

2. A tradesman turned policeman
4. It was the gravest danger
6. The Kapo who had bouts of madness
7. The Day of Atonement: Yom ___
9. Elie's inheritance was a knife and a ___
10. Elie had surgery on his ___
11. Mr. Wiesel had this ailment when he died
13. They walked here from Auschwitz
14. Elie did not do this on Yom Kippur
15. An ___ tank was at the gates of Buchenwald
17. Elie Wiesel grew up in this town
20. One Jew said he was the only one who had kept his promises
22. The prisoners ate this and soup
23. He tried to warn the Jews in Sighet: ___ the Beadle
24. Played his violin for the dying men

Down

1. Elie and his father did not stay here, but joined the evacuation
2. It ___ during the entire evacuation march
3. The only son
4. It once tasted like corpses
5. The youngest of the Wiesel children
8. They liberated the men in the hospital
9. Mr. Wiesel didn't recognize this cousin
12. Told Elie he had not been written down
13. Jewish musicians were not allowed to play this composer's music
15. The German Jew who headed the block at Buna
16. Elie's father's first name
17. Jews had to wear the yellow ___
18. The eldest of the Wiesel children
19. Dreamed of going to Haifa with Elie and Yossi
21. The Jewish New Year: ___ Hashanah
22. The next eldest of the Wiesel children

Night Crossword 2

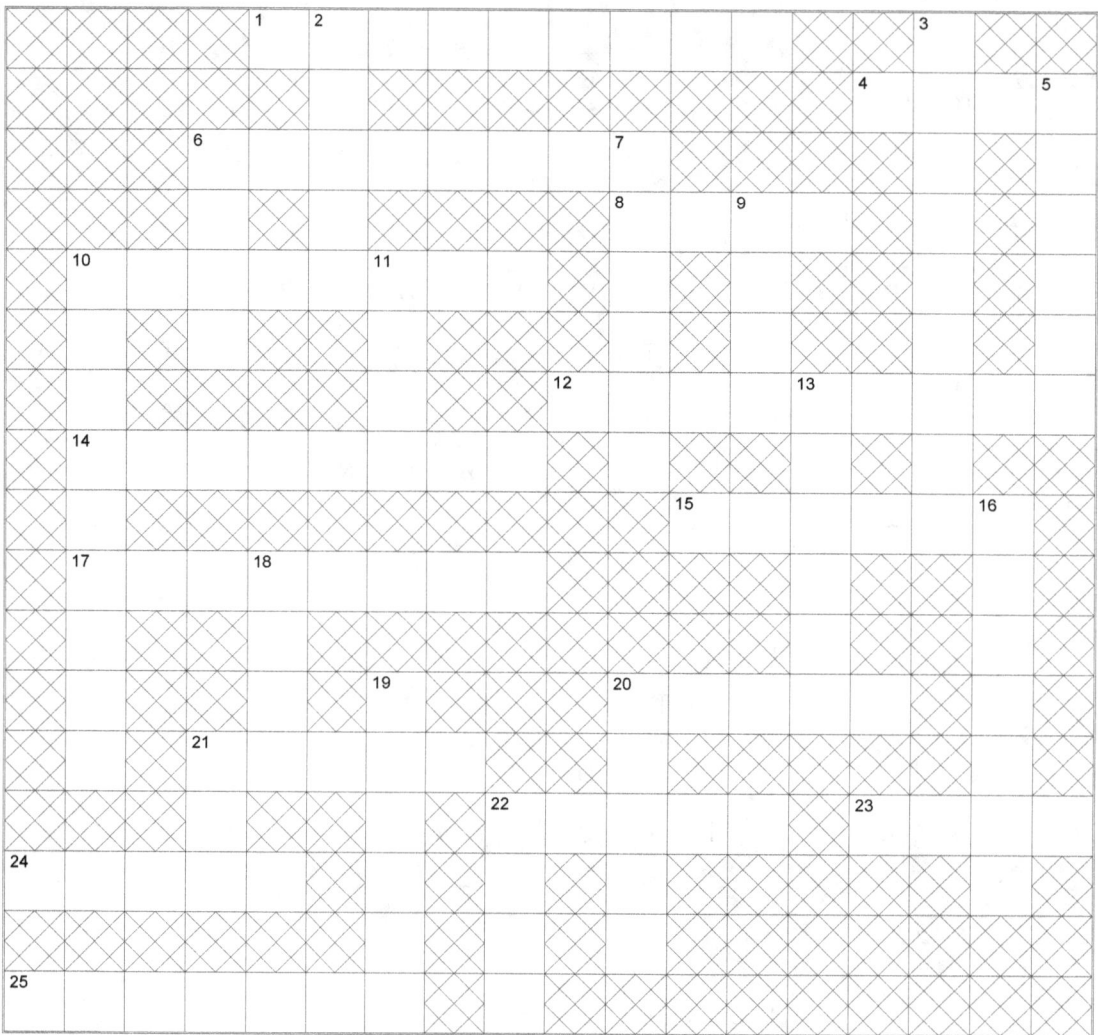

Across
1. Mr. Wiesel had this ailment when he died
4. Meir ___ died in the wagon
6. They attacked Jewish shops and synagogues
8. The Kapo who had bouts of madness
10. Elie and his father did not stay here, but joined the evacuation
12. It was the gravest danger
14. The marchers' destination
15. Played his violin for the dying men
17. They liberated the men in the hospital
20. Elie's inheritance was a knife and a ___
21. The prisoners ate this and soup
22. Mr. Wiesel didn't recognize this cousin
23. The Jewish New Year: ___ Hashanah
24. The men had to ___ the block before they evacuated
25. The youngest of the Wiesel children

Down
2. Told Elie he had not been written down
3. Elie wanted his family to move here
5. A Polish boy who was trampled during the evacuation
6. Elie did not do this on Yom Kippur
7. Elie Wiesel grew up in this town
9. The only son
10. Elie hated these police first
11. Dreamed of going to Haifa with Elie and Yossi
13. Elie's father's first name
16. The men recited this prayer for themselves
18. Jews had to wear the yellow ___
19. Offered the family safe refuge in her village
20. A tradesman turned policeman
21. The next eldest of the Wiesel children
22. It once tasted like corpses

Night Crossword 2 Answer Key

			1 D	2 Y	S	E	N	T	E	R	Y		3 P	
				O								4 K	A	5 T	Z
		6 F	A	S	C	I	S	7 S	T				L		A
			A		S			8 I	D	9 E	K		E		L
	10 H	O	S	P	I	11 T	A	L		G			S		M
	U		T			I		H		I			T		A
	N				B		12 S	E	L	13 E	C	T	I	O	N
14 G	L	E	I	W	I	T	Z		T		H		N		
A									15 J	U	L	I	E	16 K
17 R	U	18 S	S	I	A	N	S				O			A
I		T			19 M		20 S	P	O	O	N		D
A		A			M		T						D
N		21 B	R	E	A	D			22 S	T	E	I	N	23 R	O	S	H
24 C	L	E	A	N		T		O		R			H
						H		U		N			
25 T	Z	I	P	O	R	A		P					

Across
1. Mr. Wiesel had this ailment when he died
4. Meir ___ died in the wagon
6. They attacked Jewish shops and synagogues
8. The Kapo who had bouts of madness
10. Elie and his father did not stay here, but joined the evacuation
12. It was the gravest danger
14. The marchers' destination
15. Played his violin for the dying men
17. They liberated the men in the hospital
20. Elie's inheritance was a knife and a ___
21. The prisoners ate this and soup
22. Mr. Wiesel didn't recognize this cousin
23. The Jewish New Year: ___ Hashanah
24. The men had to ___ the block before they evacuated
25. The youngest of the Wiesel children

Down
2. Told Elie he had not been written down
3. Elie wanted his family to move here
5. A Polish boy who was trampled during the evacuation
6. Elie did not do this on Yom Kippur
7. Elie Wiesel grew up in this town
9. The only son
10. Elie hated these police first
11. Dreamed of going to Haifa with Elie and Yossi
13. Elie's father's first name
16. The men recited this prayer for themselves
18. Jews had to wear the yellow ___
19. Offered the family safe refuge in her village
20. A tradesman turned policeman
21. The next eldest of the Wiesel children
22. It once tasted like corpses

Night Crossword 3

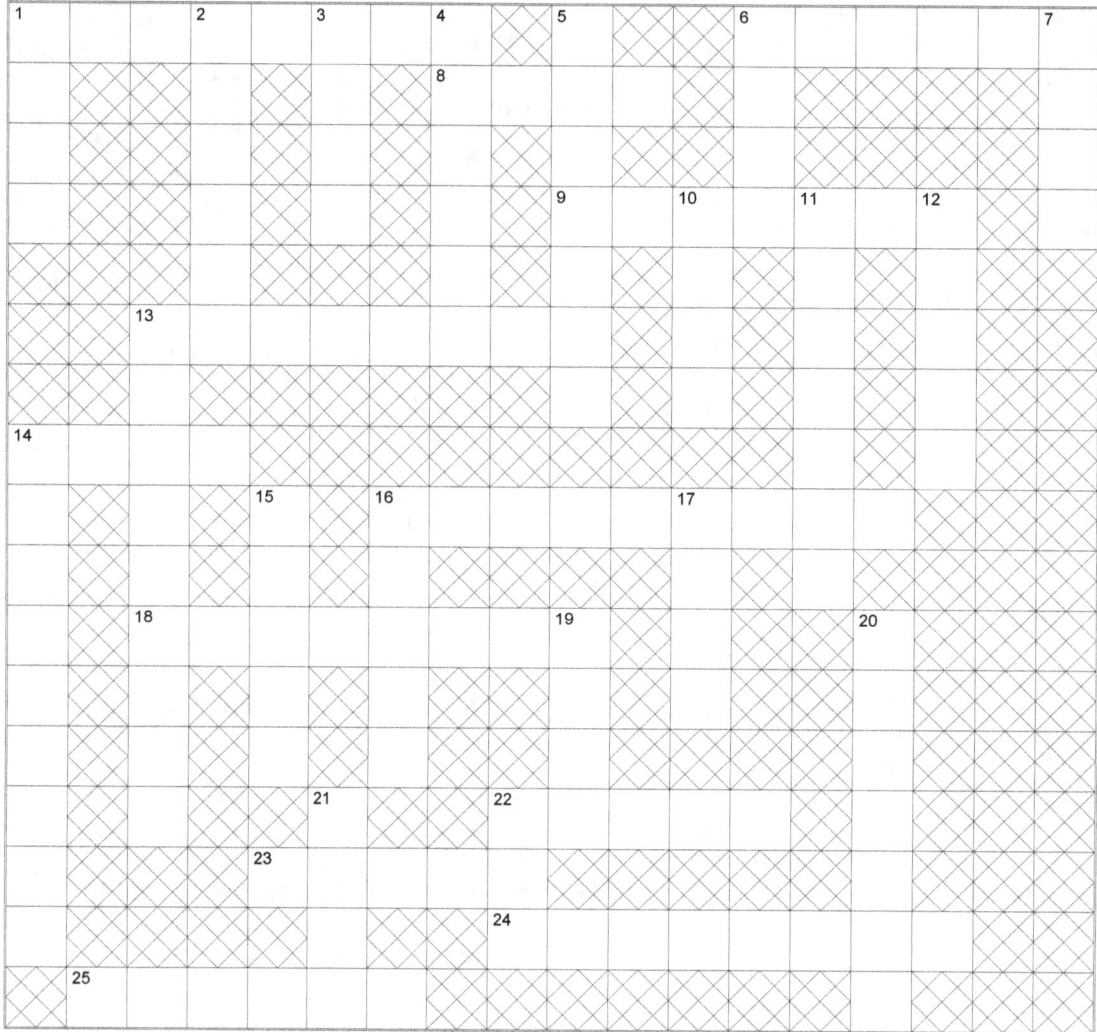

Across
1. They attacked Jewish shops and synagogues
6. He tormented Elie's father to get Elie's gold tooth
8. The Kapo who had bouts of madness
9. Two ___ were set up in Sighet
13. Elie and his father did not stay here, but joined the evacuation
14. They walked here from Auschwitz
16. Mr. Wiesel had this ailment when he died
18. They liberated the men in the hospital
22. The prisoners ate this and soup
23. He tried to warn the Jews in Sighet: ___ the Beadle
24. The German Jew who headed the block at Buna
25. Offered the family safe refuge in her village

Down
1. Elie did not do this on Yom Kippur
2. Elie's father's first name
3. It once tasted like corpses
4. Elie Wiesel grew up in this town
5. Elie saw this notorious doctor
6. Elie had surgery on his ___
7. Meir ___ died in the wagon
10. The only son
11. The youngest of the Wiesel children
12. A tradesman turned policeman
13. Elie hated these police first
14. Jewish musicians were not allowed to play this composer's music
15. Told Elie he had not been written down
16. This idea began to fascinate Elie during the evacuation
17. Dreamed of going to Haifa with Elie and Yossi
19. Jews had to wear the yellow ___
20. The men recited this prayer for themselves
21. The Jewish New Year: ___ Hashanah
22. The next eldest of the Wiesel children

Night Crossword 3 Answer Key

	F	A	S	C	I	S	T	S			M			F	R	A	N	E	K
	A		H		O		I	D	E	K				O					A
	S		L		U		G		N					O					T
	T		O		P		H		G	H	E	T	T	O	S				Z
			M				E		E		L		Z		T				
			H	O	S	P	I	T	A	L		I		I		E			
			U						E			E		P		R			
	B	U	N	A										O		N			
	E		G		Y		D	Y	S	E	N	T	E	R	Y				
	E		A		O		Y					I		A					
	T		R	U	S	S	I	A	N	S		B				K			
	H		I		S		N			T		I				A			
	O		A		I		G			A						D			
	V		N		R			B	R	E	A	D				D			
	E				M	O	S	H	E							I			
	N							A	L	P	H	O	N	S	E				
		M	A	R	T	H	A								H				

Across
1. They attacked Jewish shops and synagogues
6. He tormented Elie's father to get Elie's gold tooth
8. The Kapo who had bouts of madness
9. Two ___ were set up in Sighet
13. Elie and his father did not stay here, but joined the evacuation
14. They walked here from Auschwitz
16. Mr. Wiesel had this ailment when he died
18. They liberated the men in the hospital
22. The prisoners ate this and soup
23. He tried to warn the Jews in Sighet: ___ the Beadle
24. The German Jew who headed the block at Buna
25. Offered the family safe refuge in her village

Down
1. Elie did not do this on Yom Kippur
2. Elie's father's first name
3. It once tasted like corpses
4. Elie Wiesel grew up in this town
5. Elie saw this notorious doctor
6. Elie had surgery on his ___
7. Meir ___ died in the wagon
10. The only son
11. The youngest of the Wiesel children
12. A tradesman turned policeman
13. Elie hated these police first
14. Jewish musicians were not allowed to play this composer's music
15. Told Elie he had not been written down
16. This idea began to fascinate Elie during the evacuation
17. Dreamed of going to Haifa with Elie and Yossi
19. Jews had to wear the yellow ___
20. The men recited this prayer for themselves
21. The Jewish New Year: ___ Hashanah
22. The next eldest of the Wiesel children

Night Crossword 4

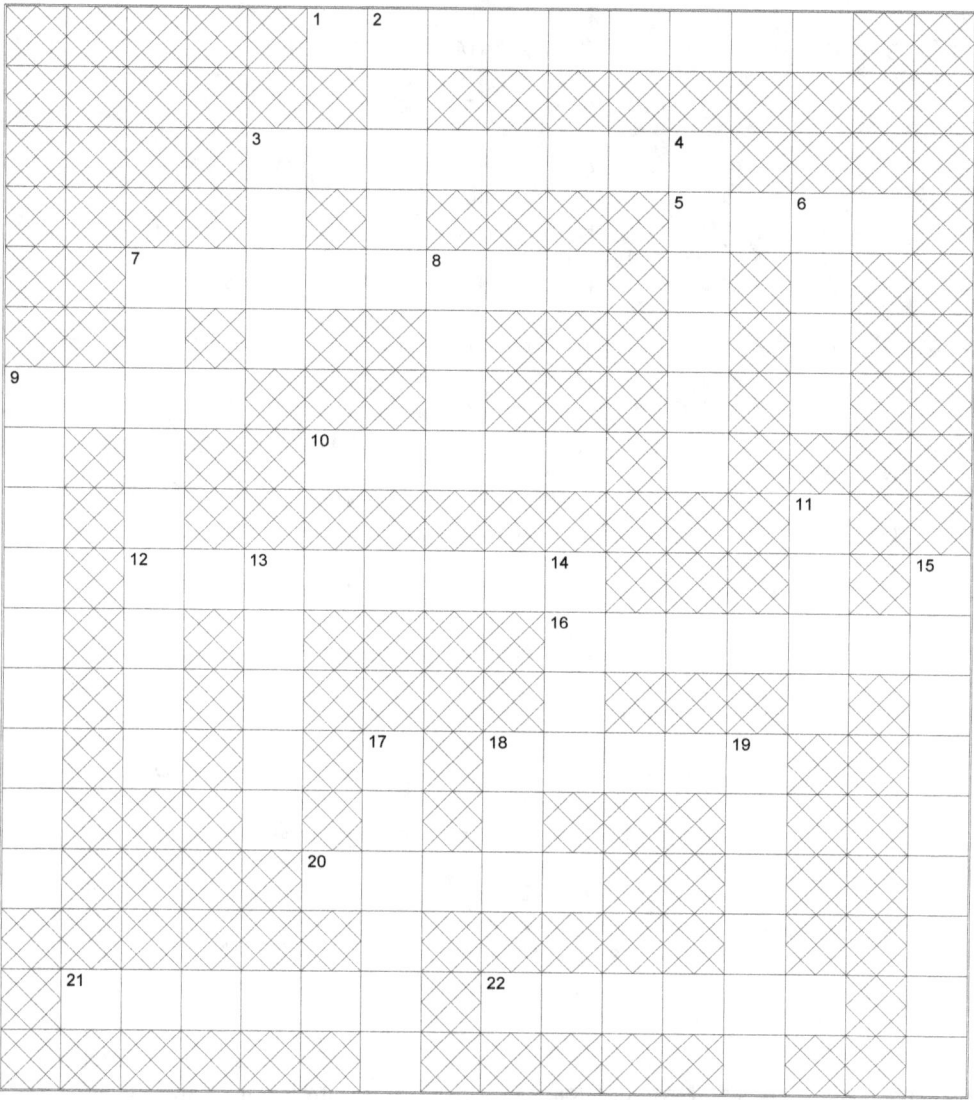

Across
1. Mr. Wiesel had this ailment when he died
3. They attacked Jewish shops and synagogues
5. The Kapo who had bouts of madness
7. Elie and his father did not stay here, but joined the evacuation
9. They walked here from Auschwitz
10. This idea began to fascinate Elie during the evacuation
12. They liberated the men in the hospital
16. The youngest of the Wiesel children
18. The prisoners ate this and soup
20. The men had to ___ the block before they evacuated
21. Offered the family safe refuge in her village
22. Played his violin for the dying men

Down
2. Told Elie he had not been written down
3. Elie did not do this on Yom Kippur
4. Elie Wiesel grew up in this town
6. The only son
7. Elie hated these police first
8. Dreamed of going to Haifa with Elie and Yossi
9. Jewish musicians were not allowed to play this composer's music
11. Elie had surgery on his ___
13. A tradesman turned policeman
14. Jews had to wear the yellow ___
15. Elie wanted his family to move here
17. A Polish boy who was trampled during the evacuation
18. The next eldest of the Wiesel children
19. Akiba ___ thought God was testing the Jews

Night Crossword 4 Answer Key

Across
1. Mr. Wiesel had this ailment when he died
3. They attacked Jewish shops and synagogues
5. The Kapo who had bouts of madness
7. Elie and his father did not stay here, but joined the evacuation
9. They walked here from Auschwitz
10. This idea began to fascinate Elie during the evacuation
12. They liberated the men in the hospital
16. The youngest of the Wiesel children
18. The prisoners ate this and soup
20. The men had to ___ the block before they evacuated
21. Offered the family safe refuge in her village
22. Played his violin for the dying men

Down
2. Told Elie he had not been written down
3. Elie did not do this on Yom Kippur
4. Elie Wiesel grew up in this town
6. The only son
7. Elie hated these police first
8. Dreamed of going to Haifa with Elie and Yossi
9. Jewish musicians were not allowed to play this composer's music
11. Elie had surgery on his ___
13. A tradesman turned policeman
14. Jews had to wear the yellow ___
15. Elie wanted his family to move here
17. A Polish boy who was trampled during the evacuation
18. The next eldest of the Wiesel children
19. Akiba ___ thought God was testing the Jews

Night

IDEK	SNOWED	HITLER	STAR	HILDA
TIBI	FASCISTS	BEA	SPOON	MARTHA
STERN	KIPPUR	FREE SPACE	FRANEK	AMERICAN
RESISTANCE	ZALMAN	TRANSYLVANIA	BUNA	DRUMER
MENGELE	SOUP	ROSH	MOSHE	KADDISH

Night

TZIPORA	DYSENTERY	ELIE	SELECTION	HUNGARIAN
KATZ	BUCHENWALD	PASSOVER	PALESTINE	YOSSI
STEIN	DYING	FREE SPACE	BEETHOVEN	GLEIWITZ
VIOLIN	GESTAPO	AUSCHWITZ	SCHACHTER	BIRKENAU
FAST	ELIAHOU	ALPHONSE	FOOT	SIGHET

Night

RUSSIANS	SELECTION	STEIN	CLEAN	GHETTOS
SPOON	PALESTINE	FOOT	HOSPITAL	KADDISH
AUSCHWITZ	BUCHENWALD	FREE SPACE	DYSENTERY	KIPPUR
DRUMER	FAST	SCHACHTER	STAR	VIOLIN
MARTHA	TIBI	ELIAHOU	GLEIWITZ	FASCISTS

Night

BEA	HITLER	BUNA	JULIEK	BREAD
ROSH	PASSOVER	MOSHE	SIGHET	FRANEK
KATZ	HILDA	FREE SPACE	HUNGARIAN	ELIE
YOSSI	TRANSYLVANIA	GESTAPO	CHLOMO	RESISTANCE
IDEK	BIRKENAU	ALPHONSE	SOUP	AMERICAN

Night

DYING	GESTAPO	BUNA	MENGELE	MARTHA
TRANSYLVANIA	GHETTOS	TZIPORA	BEA	MOSHE
KIPPUR	BREAD	FREE SPACE	DYSENTERY	SOUP
BIRKENAU	SNOWED	GLEIWITZ	SIGHET	KADDISH
IDEK	RESISTANCE	VIOLIN	HUNGARIAN	TIBI

Night

JULIEK	DRUMER	CHLOMO	PASSOVER	CLEAN
YOSSI	AUSCHWITZ	ALPHONSE	PALESTINE	FASCISTS
ELIE	SCHACHTER	FREE SPACE	RUSSIANS	HITLER
FOOT	STERN	KATZ	AMERICAN	ROSH
STEIN	SELECTION	FRANEK	HOSPITAL	BEETHOVEN

Night

ELIE	HUNGARIAN	SOUP	SIGHET	PASSOVER
KADDISH	HITLER	GLEIWITZ	STEIN	FOOT
ALPHONSE	FAST	FREE SPACE	HILDA	STERN
VIOLIN	DYING	BEA	BUCHENWALD	RESISTANCE
HOSPITAL	DRUMER	RUSSIANS	FASCISTS	KATZ

Night

CLEAN	TZIPORA	AMERICAN	KIPPUR	SELECTION
GHETTOS	MENGELE	DYSENTERY	ZALMAN	ROSH
BUNA	BREAD	FREE SPACE	STAR	BEETHOVEN
SNOWED	GESTAPO	ELIAHOU	JULIEK	PALESTINE
TRANSYLVANIA	MOSHE	SCHACHTER	MARTHA	SPOON

Night

HUNGARIAN	GLEIWITZ	BIRKENAU	VIOLIN	RESISTANCE
SPOON	FAST	HOSPITAL	GHETTOS	PALESTINE
KADDISH	FASCISTS	FREE SPACE	STAR	MARTHA
STERN	TIBI	BEA	YOSSI	SCHACHTER
AMERICAN	TRANSYLVANIA	BUCHENWALD	PASSOVER	ELIE

Night

CHLOMO	BUNA	DYSENTERY	GESTAPO	SNOWED
HILDA	CLEAN	SOUP	SELECTION	MENGELE
JULIEK	KATZ	FREE SPACE	TZIPORA	FOOT
ZALMAN	DRUMER	FRANEK	HITLER	AUSCHWITZ
KIPPUR	BREAD	DYING	STEIN	SIGHET

Night

ZALMAN	HUNGARIAN	VIOLIN	HILDA	BUNA
KIPPUR	SOUP	JULIEK	BEETHOVEN	DRUMER
CHLOMO	BIRKENAU	FREE SPACE	SNOWED	MENGELE
DYSENTERY	STERN	KADDISH	SPOON	DYING
FAST	BUCHENWALD	BEA	ALPHONSE	ELIAHOU

Night

SCHACHTER	MARTHA	GHETTOS	HOSPITAL	ROSH
HITLER	AMERICAN	KATZ	CLEAN	TIBI
TRANSYLVANIA	MOSHE	FREE SPACE	ELIE	FRANEK
YOSSI	PALESTINE	RUSSIANS	GLEIWITZ	STEIN
IDEK	STAR	PASSOVER	TZIPORA	RESISTANCE

Night

KIPPUR	SELECTION	CLEAN	STAR	BUCHENWALD
YOSSI	BUNA	RUSSIANS	GESTAPO	FASCISTS
HITLER	SOUP	FREE SPACE	HOSPITAL	BEA
MENGELE	BEETHOVEN	PALESTINE	SIGHET	BIRKENAU
AUSCHWITZ	ROSH	AMERICAN	MARTHA	IDEK

Night

RESISTANCE	TRANSYLVANIA	STEIN	STERN	GHETTOS
ZALMAN	FOOT	SNOWED	PASSOVER	VIOLIN
TZIPORA	HILDA	FREE SPACE	GLEIWITZ	FRANEK
ALPHONSE	SCHACHTER	DYSENTERY	BREAD	DRUMER
KADDISH	SPOON	KATZ	HUNGARIAN	ELIE

Night

TRANSYLVANIA	TIBI	MARTHA	HILDA	FOOT
AMERICAN	KADDISH	FRANEK	MENGELE	BEETHOVEN
SPOON	FAST	FREE SPACE	ROSH	STERN
RESISTANCE	SOUP	DYING	BEA	DRUMER
KIPPUR	SIGHET	YOSSI	BUNA	MOSHE

Night

ELIE	HOSPITAL	CHLOMO	KATZ	IDEK
RUSSIANS	FASCISTS	JULIEK	STEIN	HUNGARIAN
ZALMAN	HITLER	FREE SPACE	ELIAHOU	BREAD
ALPHONSE	VIOLIN	AUSCHWITZ	PASSOVER	SNOWED
SELECTION	BIRKENAU	CLEAN	SCHACHTER	GHETTOS

Night

HILDA	ELIE	TRANSYLVANIA	SELECTION	BEETHOVEN
STERN	SCHACHTER	PASSOVER	MENGELE	FAST
STEIN	FRANEK	FREE SPACE	GLEIWITZ	BIRKENAU
TIBI	ALPHONSE	MARTHA	IDEK	CLEAN
STAR	GESTAPO	RESISTANCE	JULIEK	KIPPUR

Night

BUNA	FASCISTS	AUSCHWITZ	BUCHENWALD	ZALMAN
HUNGARIAN	DRUMER	TZIPORA	SNOWED	RUSSIANS
GHETTOS	ELIAHOU	FREE SPACE	VIOLIN	HOSPITAL
HITLER	PALESTINE	BREAD	DYING	ROSH
CHLOMO	MOSHE	BEA	DYSENTERY	SIGHET

Night

HITLER	YOSSI	STEIN	FRANEK	RESISTANCE
MENGELE	TZIPORA	BUCHENWALD	AUSCHWITZ	FAST
ROSH	STERN	FREE SPACE	CHLOMO	GHETTOS
RUSSIANS	SIGHET	GESTAPO	JULIEK	VIOLIN
CLEAN	DYING	MOSHE	KIPPUR	TIBI

Night

SCHACHTER	ELIE	HOSPITAL	PASSOVER	BEETHOVEN
SPOON	SELECTION	HILDA	ELIAHOU	ALPHONSE
FASCISTS	KADDISH	FREE SPACE	SOUP	AMERICAN
STAR	MARTHA	PALESTINE	BIRKENAU	BUNA
FOOT	GLEIWITZ	KATZ	BEA	SNOWED

Night

GESTAPO	AUSCHWITZ	MOSHE	ELIE	FASCISTS
BIRKENAU	DYSENTERY	BUCHENWALD	BREAD	RUSSIANS
ROSH	KADDISH	FREE SPACE	FRANEK	VIOLIN
BUNA	RESISTANCE	STERN	TIBI	STAR
TRANSYLVANIA	MENGELE	HOSPITAL	DRUMER	DYING

Night

PASSOVER	FOOT	ALPHONSE	MARTHA	SOUP
GHETTOS	JULIEK	SPOON	BEETHOVEN	SELECTION
ELIAHOU	IDEK	FREE SPACE	FAST	TZIPORA
SIGHET	YOSSI	AMERICAN	PALESTINE	GLEIWITZ
CLEAN	BEA	ZALMAN	HUNGARIAN	HITLER

Night

GESTAPO	SCHACHTER	ELIAHOU	MOSHE	SNOWED
JULIEK	CLEAN	BREAD	FASCISTS	TIBI
HOSPITAL	MENGELE	FREE SPACE	MARTHA	DYSENTERY
YOSSI	TRANSYLVANIA	RUSSIANS	PALESTINE	STEIN
RESISTANCE	VIOLIN	BUNA	ZALMAN	CHLOMO

Night

TZIPORA	SELECTION	DYING	FOOT	AMERICAN
HITLER	BEETHOVEN	FAST	STAR	KIPPUR
HILDA	FRANEK	FREE SPACE	SOUP	KATZ
DRUMER	STERN	SIGHET	ROSH	PASSOVER
IDEK	GHETTOS	BIRKENAU	KADDISH	ALPHONSE

Night

JULIEK	RUSSIANS	HITLER	GESTAPO	HILDA
KIPPUR	GLEIWITZ	STAR	FAST	VIOLIN
DRUMER	HUNGARIAN	FREE SPACE	FOOT	MOSHE
BEETHOVEN	HOSPITAL	FASCISTS	AUSCHWITZ	BUCHENWALD
BREAD	SNOWED	TIBI	CLEAN	ELIAHOU

Night

YOSSI	ELIE	BEA	SOUP	ALPHONSE
AMERICAN	GHETTOS	SIGHET	ROSH	TZIPORA
KATZ	SPOON	FREE SPACE	RESISTANCE	SCHACHTER
BIRKENAU	MARTHA	PASSOVER	MENGELE	BUNA
SELECTION	TRANSYLVANIA	ZALMAN	FRANEK	STERN

Night

TZIPORA	BEETHOVEN	SIGHET	VIOLIN	IDEK
RESISTANCE	HITLER	HUNGARIAN	FOOT	JULIEK
DYSENTERY	FAST	FREE SPACE	PASSOVER	ELIE
MARTHA	KADDISH	YOSSI	CHLOMO	BUCHENWALD
CLEAN	STEIN	SOUP	HILDA	SPOON

Night

SELECTION	AUSCHWITZ	BUNA	MOSHE	ROSH
HOSPITAL	MENGELE	TRANSYLVANIA	DYING	GHETTOS
STERN	FASCISTS	FREE SPACE	SCHACHTER	ELIAHOU
PALESTINE	AMERICAN	KIPPUR	ALPHONSE	KATZ
BREAD	GLEIWITZ	GESTAPO	ZALMAN	STAR

Night

HUNGARIAN	BUCHENWALD	SELECTION	SPOON	FOOT
GESTAPO	KIPPUR	YOSSI	HOSPITAL	GHETTOS
ELIAHOU	BIRKENAU	FREE SPACE	BEETHOVEN	BEA
DRUMER	BUNA	KATZ	DYSENTERY	TIBI
STEIN	KADDISH	SCHACHTER	SIGHET	SNOWED

Night

STERN	FASCISTS	VIOLIN	SOUP	STAR
BREAD	FAST	FRANEK	HITLER	MOSHE
TRANSYLVANIA	HILDA	FREE SPACE	ALPHONSE	ELIE
JULIEK	IDEK	GLEIWITZ	CLEAN	PALESTINE
PASSOVER	ZALMAN	AUSCHWITZ	CHLOMO	MARTHA

Night

MENGELE	BEA	STERN	MARTHA	SIGHET
YOSSI	TRANSYLVANIA	GHETTOS	HUNGARIAN	KADDISH
PALESTINE	JULIEK	FREE SPACE	RUSSIANS	DRUMER
KATZ	HITLER	FAST	HILDA	ELIE
SOUP	ALPHONSE	ELIAHOU	HOSPITAL	SELECTION

Night

FOOT	TIBI	CLEAN	KIPPUR	BUNA
DYING	AMERICAN	STEIN	BUCHENWALD	PASSOVER
STAR	MOSHE	FREE SPACE	VIOLIN	FRANEK
ZALMAN	BEETHOVEN	GLEIWITZ	BREAD	SPOON
DYSENTERY	BIRKENAU	TZIPORA	IDEK	GESTAPO

Night Vocabulary Word List

No.	Word	Clue/Definition
1.	ANECDOTES	Short, humorous stories
2.	APATHY	Lack of emotion or feeling
3.	BEREAVED	Left alone by death
4.	BLANDISHMENTS	Coaxing by flattery
5.	CONSTRAINT	Restriction
6.	CONTAGION	A harmful influence
7.	CONVALESCENT	Returning to health after an illness
8.	CONVOY	A group of vehicles traveling together
9.	DEPORTEES	Those being expelled from a country
10.	DEPRIVE	To take something away from
11.	DEVOID	Completely lacking or empty
12.	DREGS	The least desirable portions
13.	ELAPSED	Passed
14.	EMACIATED	Made thin due to starvation
15.	ENCUMBERED	Hindered; restricted
16.	EVACUATION	Withdrawing troops or civilians from an area
17.	FEEBLE	Lacking strength
18.	FRENZY	Violent mental agitation or wild excitement
19.	HERMETICALLY	Sealed against the entry or escape of air
20.	INSIGNIFICANT	Trivial; not important
21.	LAMENTATION	Grief; mourning
22.	LATTER	Second of two
23.	LIVID	Ashen; pallid
24.	LUCIDITY	Clear understanding
25.	MELANCHOLY	Sadness; depression
26.	MONOCLE	An eyeglass for one eye
27.	NOTORIOUS	Known unfavorably
28.	PESTILENTIAL	Likely to cause an epidemic disease
29.	PROFOUNDLY	Absolutely; in an unqualified way
30.	PROVISIONS	Necessary supplies, such as food
31.	RAUCOUS	Boisterous and disorderly
32.	RECESSES	Remote, secret places
33.	RELENTLESSLY	Steadily; persistently
34.	SABOTAGE	Treacherous action to defeat a cause
35.	SURNAME	Family name
36.	TETHER	The limit of one's resources or endurance
37.	THRASH	Beat; hit
38.	TORMENT	To cause physical pain or mental anguish
39.	TREATISE	Written discussion of a topic
40.	VITALITY	Vigor; energy
41.	VOID	Emptiness

Night Vocabulary Fill In The Blank 1

_____

1. Boisterous and disorderly
2. Remote, secret places
3. Family name
4. Left alone by death
5. Treacherous action to defeat a cause
6. Passed
7. Known unfavorably
8. Absolutely; in an unqualified way
9. The limit of one's resources or endurance
10. A group of vehicles traveling together
11. Made thin due to starvation
12. Completely lacking or empty
13. Necessary supplies, such as food
14. The least desirable portions
15. Ashen; pallid
16. Emptiness
17. Lacking strength
18. Steadily; persistently
19. Trivial; not important
20. Beat; hit

Night Vocabulary Fill In The Blank 1 Answer Key

RAUCOUS	1. Boisterous and disorderly
RECESSES	2. Remote, secret places
SURNAME	3. Family name
BEREAVED	4. Left alone by death
SABOTAGE	5. Treacherous action to defeat a cause
ELAPSED	6. Passed
NOTORIOUS	7. Known unfavorably
PROFOUNDLY	8. Absolutely; in an unqualified way
TETHER	9. The limit of one's resources or endurance
CONVOY	10. A group of vehicles traveling together
EMACIATED	11. Made thin due to starvation
DEVOID	12. Completely lacking or empty
PROVISIONS	13. Necessary supplies, such as food
DREGS	14. The least desirable portions
LIVID	15. Ashen; pallid
VOID	16. Emptiness
FEEBLE	17. Lacking strength
RELENTLESSLY	18. Steadily; persistently
INSIGNIFICANT	19. Trivial; not important
THRASH	20. Beat; hit

Night Vocabulary Fill In The Blank 2

_____

1. Returning to health after an illness
2. Remote, secret places
3. Grief; mourning
4. Lack of emotion or feeling
5. Coaxing by flattery
6. Short, humorous stories
7. Steadily; persistently
8. The least desirable portions
9. Ashen; pallid
10. Withdrawing troops or civilians from an area
11. Lacking strength
12. A group of vehicles traveling together
13. Family name
14. Vigor; energy
15. Restriction
16. Emptiness
17. Beat; hit
18. Likely to cause an epidemic disease
19. Made thin due to starvation
20. Boisterous and disorderly

Night Vocabulary Fill In The Blank 2 Answer Key

CONVALESCENT	1. Returning to health after an illness
RECESSES	2. Remote, secret places
LAMENTATION	3. Grief; mourning
APATHY	4. Lack of emotion or feeling
BLANDISHMENTS	5. Coaxing by flattery
ANECDOTES	6. Short, humorous stories
RELENTLESSLY	7. Steadily; persistently
DREGS	8. The least desirable portions
LIVID	9. Ashen; pallid
EVACUATION	10. Withdrawing troops or civilians from an area
FEEBLE	11. Lacking strength
CONVOY	12. A group of vehicles traveling together
SURNAME	13. Family name
VITALITY	14. Vigor; energy
CONSTRAINT	15. Restriction
VOID	16. Emptiness
THRASH	17. Beat; hit
PESTILENTIAL	18. Likely to cause an epidemic disease
EMACIATED	19. Made thin due to starvation
RAUCOUS	20. Boisterous and disorderly

Night Vocabulary Fill In The Blank 3

_____

1. Treacherous action to defeat a cause
2. Family name
3. To cause physical pain or mental anguish
4. Grief; mourning
5. Violent mental agitation or wild excitement
6. To take something away from
7. Written discussion of a topic
8. Those being expelled from a country
9. Restriction
10. Boisterous and disorderly
11. Coaxing by flattery
12. An eyeglass for one eye
13. Sealed against the entry or escape of air
14. Beat; hit
15. Likely to cause an epidemic disease
16. Passed
17. Vigor; energy
18. Steadily; persistently
19. Known unfavorably
20. Lacking strength

Night Vocabulary Fill In The Blank 3 Answer Key

SABOTAGE	1. Treacherous action to defeat a cause
SURNAME	2. Family name
TORMENT	3. To cause physical pain or mental anguish
LAMENTATION	4. Grief; mourning
FRENZY	5. Violent mental agitation or wild excitement
DEPRIVE	6. To take something away from
TREATISE	7. Written discussion of a topic
DEPORTEES	8. Those being expelled from a country
CONSTRAINT	9. Restriction
RAUCOUS	10. Boisterous and disorderly
BLANDISHMENTS	11. Coaxing by flattery
MONOCLE	12. An eyeglass for one eye
HERMETICALLY	13. Sealed against the entry or escape of air
THRASH	14. Beat; hit
PESTILENTIAL	15. Likely to cause an epidemic disease
ELAPSED	16. Passed
VITALITY	17. Vigor; energy
RELENTLESSLY	18. Steadily; persistently
NOTORIOUS	19. Known unfavorably
FEEBLE	20. Lacking strength

Night Vocabulary Fill In The Blank 4

1. A harmful influence
2. Emptiness
3. Violent mental agitation or wild excitement
4. Made thin due to starvation
5. Vigor; energy
6. Absolutely; in an unqualified way
7. Withdrawing troops or civilians from an area
8. Grief; mourning
9. To cause physical pain or mental anguish
10. Sadness; depression
11. Returning to health after an illness
12. Likely to cause an epidemic disease
13. Steadily; persistently
14. The least desirable portions
15. An eyeglass for one eye
16. Necessary supplies, such as food
17. Hindered; restricted
18. Short, humorous stories
19. Clear understanding
20. Lack of emotion or feeling

Night Vocabulary Fill In The Blank 4 Answer Key

CONTAGION	1. A harmful influence
VOID	2. Emptiness
FRENZY	3. Violent mental agitation or wild excitement
EMACIATED	4. Made thin due to starvation
VITALITY	5. Vigor; energy
PROFOUNDLY	6. Absolutely; in an unqualified way
EVACUATION	7. Withdrawing troops or civilians from an area
LAMENTATION	8. Grief; mourning
TORMENT	9. To cause physical pain or mental anguish
MELANCHOLY	10. Sadness; depression
CONVALESCENT	11. Returning to health after an illness
PESTILENTIAL	12. Likely to cause an epidemic disease
RELENTLESSLY	13. Steadily; persistently
DREGS	14. The least desirable portions
MONOCLE	15. An eyeglass for one eye
PROVISIONS	16. Necessary supplies, such as food
ENCUMBERED	17. Hindered; restricted
ANECDOTES	18. Short, humorous stories
LUCIDITY	19. Clear understanding
APATHY	20. Lack of emotion or feeling

Night Vocabulary Matching 1

___ 1. DEPRIVE   A. Coaxing by flattery
___ 2. FRENZY   B. Completely lacking or empty
___ 3. BLANDISHMENTS   C. Second of two
___ 4. ANECDOTES   D. Absolutely; in an unqualified way
___ 5. PROFOUNDLY   E. Ashen; pallid
___ 6. RECESSES   F. Sadness; depression
___ 7. DREGS   G. Vigor; energy
___ 8. MELANCHOLY   H. Likely to cause an epidemic disease
___ 9. ENCUMBERED   I. A harmful influence
___10. LATTER   J. The least desirable portions
___11. PESTILENTIAL   K. To cause physical pain or mental anguish
___12. BEREAVED   L. Short, humorous stories
___13. TORMENT   M. Made thin due to starvation
___14. DEVOID   N. Hindered; restricted
___15. LIVID   O. To take something away from
___16. APATHY   P. Remote, secret places
___17. NOTORIOUS   Q. The limit of one's resources or endurance
___18. CONTAGION   R. Left alone by death
___19. MONOCLE   S. Lack of emotion or feeling
___20. LUCIDITY   T. Steadily; persistently
___21. EMACIATED   U. An eyeglass for one eye
___22. VITALITY   V. Known unfavorably
___23. DEPORTEES   W. Clear understanding
___24. RELENTLESSLY   X. Those being expelled from a country
___25. TETHER   Y. Violent mental agitation or wild excitement

Night Vocabulary Matching 1 Answer Key

O - 1. DEPRIVE	A.	Coaxing by flattery
Y - 2. FRENZY	B.	Completely lacking or empty
A - 3. BLANDISHMENTS	C.	Second of two
L - 4. ANECDOTES	D.	Absolutely; in an unqualified way
D - 5. PROFOUNDLY	E.	Ashen; pallid
P - 6. RECESSES	F.	Sadness; depression
J - 7. DREGS	G.	Vigor; energy
F - 8. MELANCHOLY	H.	Likely to cause an epidemic disease
N - 9. ENCUMBERED	I.	A harmful influence
C - 10. LATTER	J.	The least desirable portions
H - 11. PESTILENTIAL	K.	To cause physical pain or mental anguish
R - 12. BEREAVED	L.	Short, humorous stories
K - 13. TORMENT	M.	Made thin due to starvation
B - 14. DEVOID	N.	Hindered; restricted
E - 15. LIVID	O.	To take something away from
S - 16. APATHY	P.	Remote, secret places
V - 17. NOTORIOUS	Q.	The limit of one's resources or endurance
I - 18. CONTAGION	R.	Left alone by death
U - 19. MONOCLE	S.	Lack of emotion or feeling
W - 20. LUCIDITY	T.	Steadily; persistently
M - 21. EMACIATED	U.	An eyeglass for one eye
G - 22. VITALITY	V.	Known unfavorably
X - 23. DEPORTEES	W.	Clear understanding
T - 24. RELENTLESSLY	X.	Those being expelled from a country
Q - 25. TETHER	Y.	Violent mental agitation or wild excitement

Night Vocabulary Matching 2

___ 1. RAUCOUS   A. Grief; mourning
___ 2. LAMENTATION   B. Coaxing by flattery
___ 3. INSIGNIFICANT   C. Sadness; depression
___ 4. ENCUMBERED   D. Lack of emotion or feeling
___ 5. PROFOUNDLY   E. The limit of one's resources or endurance
___ 6. HERMETICALLY   F. Treacherous action to defeat a cause
___ 7. TORMENT   G. To cause physical pain or mental anguish
___ 8. SURNAME   H. Lacking strength
___ 9. DEPORTEES   I. Absolutely; in an unqualified way
___10. EVACUATION   J. Withdrawing troops or civilians from an area
___11. SABOTAGE   K. Steadily; persistently
___12. TETHER   L. Emptiness
___13. MELANCHOLY   M. Those being expelled from a country
___14. VOID   N. Family name
___15. APATHY   O. Violent mental agitation or wild excitement
___16. VITALITY   P. Sealed against the entry or escape of air
___17. FRENZY   Q. Boisterous and disorderly
___18. BEREAVED   R. Hindered; restricted
___19. PROVISIONS   S. Remote, secret places
___20. RECESSES   T. Vigor; energy
___21. FEEBLE   U. Left alone by death
___22. TREATISE   V. Trivial; not important
___23. CONVOY   W. Written discussion of a topic
___24. RELENTLESSLY   X. Necessary supplies, such as food
___25. BLANDISHMENTS   Y. A group of vehicles traveling together

Night Vocabulary Matching 2 Answer Key

Q - 1.	RAUCOUS	A. Grief; mourning
A - 2.	LAMENTATION	B. Coaxing by flattery
V - 3.	INSIGNIFICANT	C. Sadness; depression
R - 4.	ENCUMBERED	D. Lack of emotion or feeling
I - 5.	PROFOUNDLY	E. The limit of one's resources or endurance
P - 6.	HERMETICALLY	F. Treacherous action to defeat a cause
G - 7.	TORMENT	G. To cause physical pain or mental anguish
N - 8.	SURNAME	H. Lacking strength
M - 9.	DEPORTEES	I. Absolutely; in an unqualified way
J - 10.	EVACUATION	J. Withdrawing troops or civilians from an area
F - 11.	SABOTAGE	K. Steadily; persistently
E - 12.	TETHER	L. Emptiness
C - 13.	MELANCHOLY	M. Those being expelled from a country
L - 14.	VOID	N. Family name
D - 15.	APATHY	O. Violent mental agitation or wild excitement
T - 16.	VITALITY	P. Sealed against the entry or escape of air
O - 17.	FRENZY	Q. Boisterous and disorderly
U - 18.	BEREAVED	R. Hindered; restricted
X - 19.	PROVISIONS	S. Remote, secret places
S - 20.	RECESSES	T. Vigor; energy
H - 21.	FEEBLE	U. Left alone by death
W - 22.	TREATISE	V. Trivial; not important
Y - 23.	CONVOY	W. Written discussion of a topic
K - 24.	RELENTLESSLY	X. Necessary supplies, such as food
B - 25.	BLANDISHMENTS	Y. A group of vehicles traveling together

Night Vocabulary Matching 3

___ 1. LATTER   A. Trivial; not important
___ 2. CONVOY   B. Necessary supplies, such as food
___ 3. MELANCHOLY   C. Withdrawing troops or civilians from an area
___ 4. CONSTRAINT   D. Those being expelled from a country
___ 5. INSIGNIFICANT   E. The limit of one's resources or endurance
___ 6. TETHER   F. Lacking strength
___ 7. PROVISIONS   G. Left alone by death
___ 8. SURNAME   H. Violent mental agitation or wild excitement
___ 9. APATHY   I. Family name
___ 10. PROFOUNDLY   J. Sealed against the entry or escape of air
___ 11. VOID   K. Second of two
___ 12. TREATISE   L. Short, humorous stories
___ 13. FEEBLE   M. Written discussion of a topic
___ 14. HERMETICALLY   N. Hindered; restricted
___ 15. SABOTAGE   O. Steadily; persistently
___ 16. LUCIDITY   P. Beat; hit
___ 17. RELENTLESSLY   Q. Absolutely; in an unqualified way
___ 18. ANECDOTES   R. Treacherous action to defeat a cause
___ 19. THRASH   S. Emptiness
___ 20. LAMENTATION   T. Grief; mourning
___ 21. FRENZY   U. Sadness; depression
___ 22. DEPORTEES   V. Lack of emotion or feeling
___ 23. EVACUATION   W. Clear understanding
___ 24. BEREAVED   X. Restriction
___ 25. ENCUMBERED   Y. A group of vehicles traveling together

Night Vocabulary Matching 3 Answer Key

K - 1. LATTER		A. Trivial; not important
Y - 2. CONVOY		B. Necessary supplies, such as food
U - 3. MELANCHOLY		C. Withdrawing troops or civilians from an area
X - 4. CONSTRAINT		D. Those being expelled from a country
A - 5. INSIGNIFICANT		E. The limit of one's resources or endurance
E - 6. TETHER		F. Lacking strength
B - 7. PROVISIONS		G. Left alone by death
I - 8. SURNAME		H. Violent mental agitation or wild excitement
V - 9. APATHY		I. Family name
Q - 10. PROFOUNDLY		J. Sealed against the entry or escape of air
S - 11. VOID		K. Second of two
M - 12. TREATISE		L. Short, humorous stories
F - 13. FEEBLE		M. Written discussion of a topic
J - 14. HERMETICALLY		N. Hindered; restricted
R - 15. SABOTAGE		O. Steadily; persistently
W - 16. LUCIDITY		P. Beat; hit
O - 17. RELENTLESSLY		Q. Absolutely; in an unqualified way
L - 18. ANECDOTES		R. Treacherous action to defeat a cause
P - 19. THRASH		S. Emptiness
T - 20. LAMENTATION		T. Grief; mourning
H - 21. FRENZY		U. Sadness; depression
D - 22. DEPORTEES		V. Lack of emotion or feeling
C - 23. EVACUATION		W. Clear understanding
G - 24. BEREAVED		X. Restriction
N - 25. ENCUMBERED		Y. A group of vehicles traveling together

Night Vocabulary Matching 4

___ 1. ANECDOTES   A. A group of vehicles traveling together
___ 2. CONVOY   B. Sadness; depression
___ 3. LUCIDITY   C. Second of two
___ 4. TORMENT   D. Returning to health after an illness
___ 5. LATTER   E. A harmful influence
___ 6. THRASH   F. Absolutely; in an unqualified way
___ 7. FEEBLE   G. Necessary supplies, such as food
___ 8. LAMENTATION   H. Left alone by death
___ 9. CONVALESCENT   I. To cause physical pain or mental anguish
___10. BLANDISHMENTS   J. Lacking strength
___11. ELAPSED   K. Grief; mourning
___12. EMACIATED   L. Clear understanding
___13. VOID   M. Vigor; energy
___14. HERMETICALLY   N. Made thin due to starvation
___15. TREATISE   O. Restriction
___16. PROFOUNDLY   P. Short, humorous stories
___17. NOTORIOUS   Q. Beat; hit
___18. PROVISIONS   R. Written discussion of a topic
___19. RECESSES   S. The limit of one's resources or endurance
___20. BEREAVED   T. Passed
___21. CONTAGION   U. Known unfavorably
___22. CONSTRAINT   V. Sealed against the entry or escape of air
___23. TETHER   W. Coaxing by flattery
___24. VITALITY   X. Remote, secret places
___25. MELANCHOLY   Y. Emptiness

Night Vocabulary Matching 4 Answer Key

P - 1. ANECDOTES	A.	A group of vehicles traveling together
A - 2. CONVOY	B.	Sadness; depression
L - 3. LUCIDITY	C.	Second of two
I - 4. TORMENT	D.	Returning to health after an illness
C - 5. LATTER	E.	A harmful influence
Q - 6. THRASH	F.	Absolutely; in an unqualified way
J - 7. FEEBLE	G.	Necessary supplies, such as food
K - 8. LAMENTATION	H.	Left alone by death
D - 9. CONVALESCENT	I.	To cause physical pain or mental anguish
W - 10. BLANDISHMENTS	J.	Lacking strength
T - 11. ELAPSED	K.	Grief; mourning
N - 12. EMACIATED	L.	Clear understanding
Y - 13. VOID	M.	Vigor; energy
V - 14. HERMETICALLY	N.	Made thin due to starvation
R - 15. TREATISE	O.	Restriction
F - 16. PROFOUNDLY	P.	Short, humorous stories
U - 17. NOTORIOUS	Q.	Beat; hit
G - 18. PROVISIONS	R.	Written discussion of a topic
X - 19. RECESSES	S.	The limit of one's resources or endurance
H - 20. BEREAVED	T.	Passed
E - 21. CONTAGION	U.	Known unfavorably
O - 22. CONSTRAINT	V.	Sealed against the entry or escape of air
S - 23. TETHER	W.	Coaxing by flattery
M - 24. VITALITY	X.	Remote, secret places
B - 25. MELANCHOLY	Y.	Emptiness

Night Vocabulary Magic Squares 1

Match the definition with the vocabulary word. Put your answers in the magic squares below. When your answers are correct, all columns and rows will add to the same number.

A. ANECDOTES
B. MELANCHOLY
C. HERMETICALLY
D. LIVID
E. CONVALESCENT
F. FEEBLE
G. CONTAGION
H. SURNAME
I. PESTILENTIAL
J. TETHER
K. ENCUMBERED
L. ELAPSED
M. RAUCOUS
N. NOTORIOUS
O. TORMENT
P. DEPRIVE

1. Family name
2. Boisterous and disorderly
3. Sadness; depression
4. Hindered; restricted
5. The limit of one's resources or endurance
6. Sealed against the entry or escape of air
7. To take something away from
8. Returning to health after an illness
9. To cause physical pain or mental anguish
10. Lacking strength
11. Likely to cause an epidemic disease
12. Ashen; pallid
13. Short, humorous stories
14. Passed
15. A harmful influence
16. Known unfavorably

A=	B=	C=	D=
E=	F=	G=	H=
I=	J=	K=	L=
M=	N=	O=	P=

Night Vocabulary Magic Squares 1 Answer Key

Match the definition with the vocabulary word. Put your answers in the magic squares below. When your answers are correct, all columns and rows will add to the same number.

A. ANECDOTES
B. MELANCHOLY
C. HERMETICALLY
D. LIVID
E. CONVALESCENT
F. FEEBLE
G. CONTAGION
H. SURNAME
I. PESTILENTIAL
J. TETHER
K. ENCUMBERED
L. ELAPSED
M. RAUCOUS
N. NOTORIOUS
O. TORMENT
P. DEPRIVE

1. Family name
2. Boisterous and disorderly
3. Sadness; depression
4. Hindered; restricted
5. The limit of one's resources or endurance
6. Sealed against the entry or escape of air
7. To take something away from
8. Returning to health after an illness
9. To cause physical pain or mental anguish
10. Lacking strength
11. Likely to cause an epidemic disease
12. Ashen; pallid
13. Short, humorous stories
14. Passed
15. A harmful influence
16. Known unfavorably

A=13	B=3	C=6	D=12
E=8	F=10	G=15	H=1
I=11	J=5	K=4	L=14
M=2	N=16	O=9	P=7

Night Vocabulary Magic Squares 2

Match the definition with the vocabulary word. Put your answers in the magic squares below. When your answers are correct, all columns and rows will add to the same number.

A. DREGS
B. DEVOID
C. THRASH
D. BLANDISHMENTS
E. FRENZY
F. VITALITY
G. RECESSES
H. EVACUATION
I. EMACIATED
J. FEEBLE
K. TORMENT
L. RELENTLESSLY
M. SABOTAGE
N. PESTILENTIAL
O. CONTAGION
P. APATHY

1. The least desirable portions
2. Likely to cause an epidemic disease
3. Lacking strength
4. Violent mental agitation or wild excitement
5. Remote, secret places
6. Steadily; persistently
7. Lack of emotion or feeling
8. Beat; hit
9. A harmful influence
10. Coaxing by flattery
11. Withdrawing troops or civilians from an area
12. To cause physical pain or mental anguish
13. Made thin due to starvation
14. Vigor; energy
15. Completely lacking or empty
16. Treacherous action to defeat a cause

A=	B=	C=	D=
E=	F=	G=	H=
I=	J=	K=	L=
M=	N=	O=	P=

Night Vocabulary Magic Squares 2 Answer Key

Match the definition with the vocabulary word. Put your answers in the magic squares below. When your answers are correct, all columns and rows will add to the same number.

A. DREGS
B. DEVOID
C. THRASH
D. BLANDISHMENTS
E. FRENZY
F. VITALITY
G. RECESSES
H. EVACUATION
I. EMACIATED
J. FEEBLE
K. TORMENT
L. RELENTLESSLY
M. SABOTAGE
N. PESTILENTIAL
O. CONTAGION
P. APATHY

1. The least desirable portions
2. Likely to cause an epidemic disease
3. Lacking strength
4. Violent mental agitation or wild excitement
5. Remote, secret places
6. Steadily; persistently
7. Lack of emotion or feeling
8. Beat; hit
9. A harmful influence
10. Coaxing by flattery
11. Withdrawing troops or civilians from an area
12. To cause physical pain or mental anguish
13. Made thin due to starvation
14. Vigor; energy
15. Completely lacking or empty
16. Treacherous action to defeat a cause

A=1	B=15	C=8	D=10
E=4	F=14	G=5	H=11
I=13	J=3	K=12	L=6
M=16	N=2	O=9	P=7

Night Vocabulary Magic Squares 3

Match the definition with the vocabulary word. Put your answers in the magic squares below. When your answers are correct, all columns and rows will add to the same number.

A. FEEBLE
B. SURNAME
C. DEVOID
D. CONTAGION
E. RELENTLESSLY
F. MONOCLE
G. RAUCOUS
H. CONVOY
I. VITALITY
J. ANECDOTES
K. LATTER
L. APATHY
M. EMACIATED
N. NOTORIOUS
O. LUCIDITY
P. INSIGNIFICANT

1. Clear understanding
2. A harmful influence
3. Short, humorous stories
4. Steadily; persistently
5. Vigor; energy
6. An eyeglass for one eye
7. Trivial; not important
8. Completely lacking or empty
9. A group of vehicles traveling together
10. Second of two
11. Lacking strength
12. Known unfavorably
13. Family name
14. Made thin due to starvation
15. Boisterous and disorderly
16. Lack of emotion or feeling

A= 11	B= 13	C= 8	D= 2
E= 4	F= 6	G= 15	H= 9
I= 5	J= 3	K= 10	L= 16
M= 14	N= 12	O= 1	P= 7

Night Vocabulary Magic Squares 3 Answer Key

Match the definition with the vocabulary word. Put your answers in the magic squares below. When your answers are correct, all columns and rows will add to the same number.

A. FEEBLE
B. SURNAME
C. DEVOID
D. CONTAGION
E. RELENTLESSLY
F. MONOCLE
G. RAUCOUS
H. CONVOY
I. VITALITY
J. ANECDOTES
K. LATTER
L. APATHY
M. EMACIATED
N. NOTORIOUS
O. LUCIDITY
P. INSIGNIFICANT

1. Clear understanding
2. A harmful influence
3. Short, humorous stories
4. Steadily; persistently
5. Vigor; energy
6. An eyeglass for one eye
7. Trivial; not important
8. Completely lacking or empty
9. A group of vehicles traveling together
10. Second of two
11. Lacking strength
12. Known unfavorably
13. Family name
14. Made thin due to starvation
15. Boisterous and disorderly
16. Lack of emotion or feeling

A=11	B=13	C=8	D=2
E=4	F=6	G=15	H=9
I=5	J=3	K=10	L=16
M=14	N=12	O=1	P=7

Night Vocabulary Magic Squares 4

Match the definition with the vocabulary word. Put your answers in the magic squares below. When your answers are correct, all columns and rows will add to the same number.

A. ELAPSED
B. LIVID
C. CONTAGION
D. MONOCLE
E. VITALITY
F. LATTER
G. EMACIATED
H. BLANDISHMENTS
I. APATHY
J. DEPRIVE
K. DEPORTEES
L. HERMETICALLY
M. TETHER
N. CONSTRAINT
O. FRENZY
P. VOID

1. Coaxing by flattery
2. Passed
3. Ashen; pallid
4. Made thin due to starvation
5. To take something away from
6. Violent mental agitation or wild excitement
7. Emptiness
8. Lack of emotion or feeling
9. Those being expelled from a country
10. Restriction
11. The limit of one's resources or endurance
12. Sealed against the entry or escape of air
13. Vigor; energy
14. An eyeglass for one eye
15. A harmful influence
16. Second of two

A=	B=	C=	D=
E=	F=	G=	H=
I=	J=	K=	L=
M=	N=	O=	P=

Night Vocabulary Magic Squares 4 Answer Key

Match the definition with the vocabulary word. Put your answers in the magic squares below. When your answers are correct, all columns and rows will add to the same number.

A. ELAPSED
B. LIVID
C. CONTAGION
D. MONOCLE
E. VITALITY
F. LATTER
G. EMACIATED
H. BLANDISHMENTS
I. APATHY
J. DEPRIVE
K. DEPORTEES
L. HERMETICALLY
M. TETHER
N. CONSTRAINT
O. FRENZY
P. VOID

1. Coaxing by flattery
2. Passed
3. Ashen; pallid
4. Made thin due to starvation
5. To take something away from
6. Violent mental agitation or wild excitement
7. Emptiness
8. Lack of emotion or feeling
9. Those being expelled from a country
10. Restriction
11. The limit of one's resources or endurance
12. Sealed against the entry or escape of air
13. Vigor; energy
14. An eyeglass for one eye
15. A harmful influence
16. Second of two

A=2	B=3	C=15	D=14
E=13	F=16	G=4	H=1
I=8	J=5	K=9	L=12
M=11	N=10	O=6	P=7

Night Vocabulary Word Search 1

```
E L C O N O M V S U O C U A R E X Y P P C E V P R
N Z C G R Y J E F A N K G G V K T L R E O L R N
C E J O D C S Z J N B H M I S I R L O S N A T O Q
U K M Y N S R X Y K J O R E D E E A V T T P A F C
M B T A E S M G S Q R P T I V L A C I I A S L O M
B N L C C W T E T K E O C A Q A T I S L G E I U T
E P E A V I E R F D D U C W G M I T I E I D T N G
R R G L N T A L A C L U N B K E S E O N O M Y D K
E H Z M R D F T E I A D D V F N E M N T N V L L M
D S Y O B L I N E T N R H B S T X R S I M Y S Y X
Y P P Y W G A S I D B T G N R A Z E X A S L S X P
S E P S V H D O H G W F M T T M H K L X J E Z S
D P N L C N T R M Y P D V P I C D W P Z M L I Q
C M W W Z W G K Q L E S C X V O F M Q Z L C T N Q
F F R S Q H K P N Z Y N P G T N C H R Q O Q N S L
D W C G W B G G Y X V X T H Q S L D H N H K E I Z
X G G P B F W B B N T F D S R S V S V P H Z L G G
M L D T L K E Z R S N Z X Z U Y J A V N F B E N Z
B G W W T R X R K G V T S O T X L B Q N S M R I W
L P W P E S T Y Y A H O I J T E L S L U D Q X F C
I L D A T T B Z O P R R C M S H D A R R I T W I S
V Y V V H Z N Q V A O M T C Z Z R N T C O Z X C J
I E H W E E Y H N T Z E E N Y W A A P T V S L A M
D I O V R X Y L O H C N A L E M N H S G E R D N V
V S Q F P W V N C Y T T F E E B L E R H D R W T L
```

A group of vehicles traveling together (6)
A harmful influence (9)
Absolutely; in an unqualified way (10)
An eyeglass for one eye (7)
Ashen; pallid (5)
Beat; hit (6)
Boisterous and disorderly (7)
Clear understanding (8)
Coaxing by flattery (13)
Completely lacking or empty (6)
Emptiness (4)
Family name (7)
Grief; mourning (11)
Hindered; restricted (10)
Known unfavorably (9)
Lack of emotion or feeling (6)
Lacking strength (6)
Left alone by death (8)
Likely to cause an epidemic disease (12)
Made thin due to starvation (9)
Necessary supplies, such as food (10)
Passed (7)

Remote, secret places (8)
Restriction (10)
Returning to health after an illness (12)
Sadness; depression (10)
Sealed against the entry or escape of air (12)
Second of two (6)
Short, humorous stories (9)
Steadily; persistently (12)
The least desirable portions (5)
The limit of one's resources or endurance (6)
Those being expelled from a country (9)
To cause physical pain or mental anguish (7)
To take something away from (7)
Treacherous action to defeat a cause (8)
Trivial; not important (13)
Vigor; energy (8)
Violent mental agitation or wild excitement (6)
Withdrawing troops or civilians from an area (10)
Written discussion of a topic (8)

Night Vocabulary Word Search 1 Answer Key

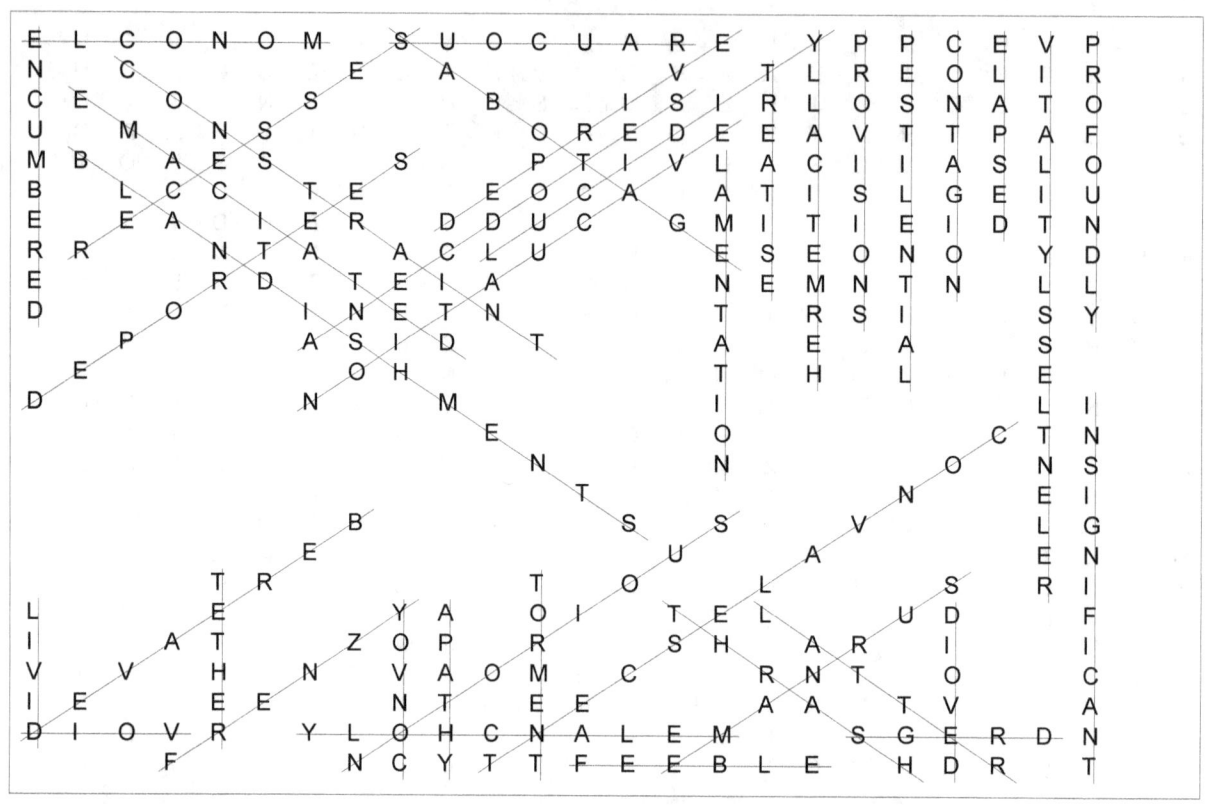

A group of vehicles traveling together (6)
A harmful influence (9)
Absolutely; in an unqualified way (10)
An eyeglass for one eye (7)
Ashen; pallid (5)
Beat; hit (6)
Boisterous and disorderly (7)
Clear understanding (8)
Coaxing by flattery (13)
Completely lacking or empty (6)
Emptiness (4)
Family name (7)
Grief; mourning (11)
Hindered; restricted (10)
Known unfavorably (9)
Lack of emotion or feeling (6)
Lacking strength (6)
Left alone by death (8)
Likely to cause an epidemic disease (12)
Made thin due to starvation (9)
Necessary supplies, such as food (10)
Passed (7)

Remote, secret places (8)
Restriction (10)
Returning to health after an illness (12)
Sadness; depression (10)
Sealed against the entry or escape of air (12)
Second of two (6)
Short, humorous stories (9)
Steadily; persistently (12)
The least desirable portions (5)
The limit of one's resources or endurance (6)
Those being expelled from a country (9)
To cause physical pain or mental anguish (7)
To take something away from (7)
Treacherous action to defeat a cause (8)
Trivial; not important (13)
Vigor; energy (8)
Violent mental agitation or wild excitement (6)
Withdrawing troops or civilians from an area (10)
Written discussion of a topic (8)

Night Vocabulary Word Search 2

```
V S U R N A M E C O N S T R A I N T Y E E F M L S
I H J S P J D F J X S V H H G O N N L B L R N I F
T C M S W X Z C V M V T H B I D P B D Q A E F V S
A K L Y L W R S O L W P M T P Z E A N R P N G I G
L P R O V I S I O N S P A B C E Z P U Z S Z N D D
I D I W V K B M J M V U Z F F M K A O D E Y V K Y
T E W N Q D H H T B C A T Z Q Q B T F N D C Y X Y
Y R D F S N D F E A D N L Z J J V H O D V L L B R
Z E G R L I Z K V R H Z Z E C Q T Y R W S L A D V
Q B K X T Q G E Z W M C F E S L C F P S C D M G L
W M F W Q P V N Y R X E M Q X C L K E Z Z E E S Z
Z U S T L Q T V I G E A T W F Y E L C C X P N A H
T C Q S K L Q F N F C C R I G L T N C Y T O T B P
P N S L S W Z O Y I I V E Z C N G C T V H R A O Q
S E V V N S I H A Q H C M S E A G T T F R T T T V
W N S J T G V T V D Z B A L S H L D E H A E I A Q
Z P O T A J E G Q R M E E N X E C L B T S E O G D
T Q Y T I D I C U L T R E A T I S E Y R H S N E W
J O N L O L J L G Z N E R N H G V O E D U E V L G
X O R B R R E Z M W F A L J E I V T F O P O R C R
C C R M F F I N R C Q V J R R N T X C J I Q N O W
D Q A N E C D O T E S E D P O A Y U M D I O V N Q
C P R J H N B K U I H D E C L Z A D V Y W J G O Q
C T D F L X T G V S A D X M Q R K C P M J W W M Z
M E L A N C H O L Y B L A N D I S H M E N T S F C
```

A group of vehicles traveling together (6)
A harmful influence (9)
Absolutely; in an unqualified way (10)
An eyeglass for one eye (7)
Ashen; pallid (5)
Beat; hit (6)
Boisterous and disorderly (7)
Clear understanding (8)
Coaxing by flattery (13)
Completely lacking or empty (6)
Emptiness (4)
Family name (7)
Grief; mourning (11)
Hindered; restricted (10)
Known unfavorably (9)
Lack of emotion or feeling (6)
Lacking strength (6)
Left alone by death (8)
Likely to cause an epidemic disease (12)
Made thin due to starvation (9)
Necessary supplies, such as food (10)
Passed (7)

Remote, secret places (8)
Restriction (10)
Returning to health after an illness (12)
Sadness; depression (10)
Sealed against the entry or escape of air (12)
Second of two (6)
Short, humorous stories (9)
Steadily; persistently (12)
The least desirable portions (5)
The limit of one's resources or endurance (6)
Those being expelled from a country (9)
To cause physical pain or mental anguish (7)
To take something away from (7)
Treacherous action to defeat a cause (8)
Trivial; not important (13)
Vigor; energy (8)
Violent mental agitation or wild excitement (6)
Withdrawing troops or civilians from an area (10)
Written discussion of a topic (8)

Night Vocabulary Word Search 2 Answer Key

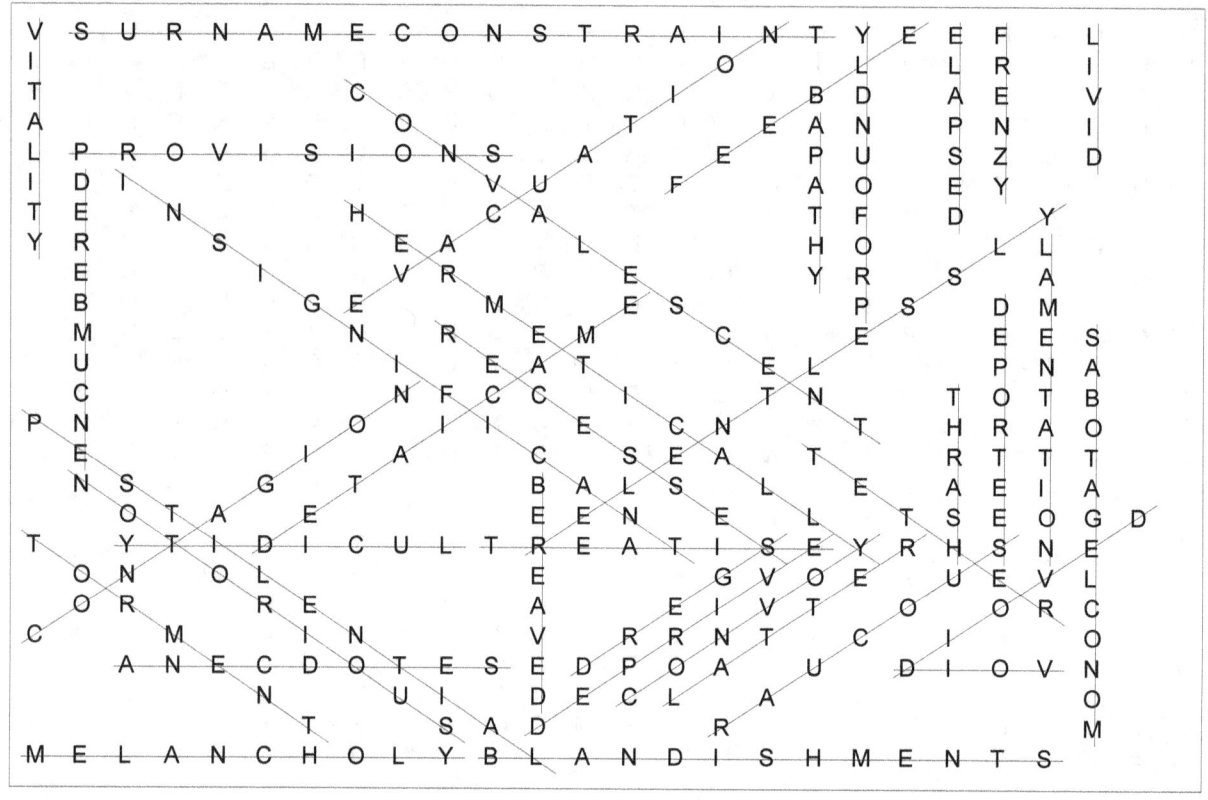

A group of vehicles traveling together (6)
A harmful influence (9)
Absolutely; in an unqualified way (10)
An eyeglass for one eye (7)
Ashen; pallid (5)
Beat; hit (6)
Boisterous and disorderly (7)
Clear understanding (8)
Coaxing by flattery (13)
Completely lacking or empty (6)
Emptiness (4)
Family name (7)
Grief; mourning (11)
Hindered; restricted (10)
Known unfavorably (9)
Lack of emotion or feeling (6)
Lacking strength (6)
Left alone by death (8)
Likely to cause an epidemic disease (12)
Made thin due to starvation (9)
Necessary supplies, such as food (10)
Passed (7)

Remote, secret places (8)
Restriction (10)
Returning to health after an illness (12)
Sadness; depression (10)
Sealed against the entry or escape of air (12)
Second of two (6)
Short, humorous stories (9)
Steadily; persistently (12)
The least desirable portions (5)
The limit of one's resources or endurance (6)
Those being expelled from a country (9)
To cause physical pain or mental anguish (7)
To take something away from (7)
Treacherous action to defeat a cause (8)
Trivial; not important (13)
Vigor; energy (8)
Violent mental agitation or wild excitement (6)
Withdrawing troops or civilians from an area (10)
Written discussion of a topic (8)

Night Vocabulary Word Search 3

```
H E R M E T I C A L L Y P V T L P K R S M P W X X
P P V C O N V A L E S C E N T Z R D A J E W K N C
N P R N K K F K H W H T S S N J O B U W L Y C X X
B D X O F V D S H Q K P T K C T V G C J A V T S B
S U O I R O T O N N J L I W S O I X O R N Y R Y F
L T K T Z D R W L R H T L Z W R S R U L C P P E M
S H Y A X V R Y W L N G E W H M I G S R H R S M X
Q L W T J H B E H L I S N V W E O B Y T O Y A A Z
C J B N N R Y N G G E V T N I N N L B F L O B C Z
L R R E C E S S E S T N I A R T S N O C Y V O I D
Y B L M R W Q L I Q D N A D N S A U F S F N T A L
F H Q A Q E L T Q E S E L Q E E N L R E N O A T N
J M B L Z P A H G I V Z P L J D C Y I N E C G E Q
Q L A T T E R V G Y M A T O L R F D Y T A B E D J
C P N X R H L N E W J N C Y R T Y Z O S Y M L D Y
C O D T L R I A K D E R J U J T N T B T R C E E Q
T J N J D F C Q P L W K R C A E E F C E E L D B X
S H L T I E J C E S A C W S R T W E H G C S V Y C
C L R C A R P R Z G E P S F C C I T S O Q L T L D
G J A A Z G M R M K Q D A H J B E O N J B I P D F
Y N Q Z S X I B I D X E R T Q T G O N W D B F J J
T B M Z M H T O B V X V S H H B M X Z I N V M Y D
N X D G D T G W N V E O P W M Y M Z C S Z N Y M L
V T V L T H T C K Z L I G W E N C U M B E R E D F
R R G S T N E M H S I D N A L B L X Y T J H C S K
```

ANECDOTES	DREGS	LIVID	SABOTAGE
APATHY	ELAPSED	LUCIDITY	SURNAME
BEREAVED	EMACIATED	MELANCHOLY	TETHER
BLANDISHMENTS	ENCUMBERED	MONOCLE	THRASH
CONSTRAINT	EVACUATION	NOTORIOUS	TORMENT
CONTAGION	FEEBLE	PESTILENTIAL	TREATISE
CONVALESCENT	FRENZY	PROFOUNDLY	VITALITY
CONVOY	HERMETICALLY	PROVISIONS	VOID
DEPORTEES	INSIGNIFICANT	RAUCOUS	
DEPRIVE	LAMENTATION	RECESSES	
DEVOID	LATTER	RELENTLESSLY	

Night Vocabulary Word Search 3 Answer Key

ANECDOTES	DREGS	LIVID	SABOTAGE
APATHY	ELAPSED	LUCIDITY	SURNAME
BEREAVED	EMACIATED	MELANCHOLY	TETHER
BLANDISHMENTS	ENCUMBERED	MONOCLE	THRASH
CONSTRAINT	EVACUATION	NOTORIOUS	TORMENT
CONTAGION	FEEBLE	PESTILENTIAL	TREATISE
CONVALESCENT	FRENZY	PROFOUNDLY	VITALITY
CONVOY	HERMETICALLY	PROVISIONS	VOID
DEPORTEES	INSIGNIFICANT	RAUCOUS	
DEPRIVE	LAMENTATION	RECESSES	
DEVOID	LATTER	RELENTLESSLY	

Night Vocabulary Word Search 4

```
P E S T I L E N T I A L N O T O R I O U S V F Q N
F D W Z G P G F P Y C G G Q C O N S T R A I N T G C
W B E D B M N K F W Y J H R Y P B Z S X B Q D L B
F K S P D K Z T X J N S Y L S S E L T N E L E R W
X F K D O J D F D O B F X T K T W Q X D D Z R T T
Y V G E F R F L I F N L S S X N Y D C J D D E S M
H F Y L J L T G T Z E U L B V N L B Z E G C B N T
S B R C Y D A E H L O E Y F R H T Z V J B W M Z N
E A W O K T S L E C D X B W T S V A P H E N U P R
L V B N N X D T U S E W D L P A E O V V H M C T D
A R Q O V I T A L I T Y Z N E R F T I Y O V N O C
P N C M T V R N P G A L L H E H O R O D T E E Q G
S F P I T A D C V J I L H B J T P V C R C M S N N
E L M N H X G M R D C A W B L E A G I S M T Q V N
D A E S I T A E R T A C C G D I H N E S N E N H F
G T L I A Z D E E C M I P L X J V L E E I O N B P
W T A G P B G Y H R E T K R G F A I M C I O B T W
J E N N A S X W T D Z E E M O V N H D T D P N G C
W R C I T Z P R E F C M P L N F S X A B K O J S V
K W H F H H F V T G A R F O G I O T J F G J T M P
X Z O I Y F O Q K N Z E C N D T N U F V N C J E G
H H L C D I Y D R H Y H J N S E Z T N X F N S X S
C V Y A D Z K U C P M N A T M L U C I D I T Y Z M
N H Q N M M S V K H G L M A P C Y S H B L V F T X
N O I T A U C A V E B D L R E C E S S E S Y H L X
```

ANECDOTES	DREGS	LIVID	SABOTAGE
APATHY	ELAPSED	LUCIDITY	SURNAME
BEREAVED	EMACIATED	MELANCHOLY	TETHER
BLANDISHMENTS	ENCUMBERED	MONOCLE	THRASH
CONSTRAINT	EVACUATION	NOTORIOUS	TORMENT
CONTAGION	FEEBLE	PESTILENTIAL	TREATISE
CONVALESCENT	FRENZY	PROFOUNDLY	VITALITY
CONVOY	HERMETICALLY	PROVISIONS	VOID
DEPORTEES	INSIGNIFICANT	RAUCOUS	
DEPRIVE	LAMENTATION	RECESSES	
DEVOID	LATTER	RELENTLESSLY	

Night Vocabulary Word Search 4 Answer Key

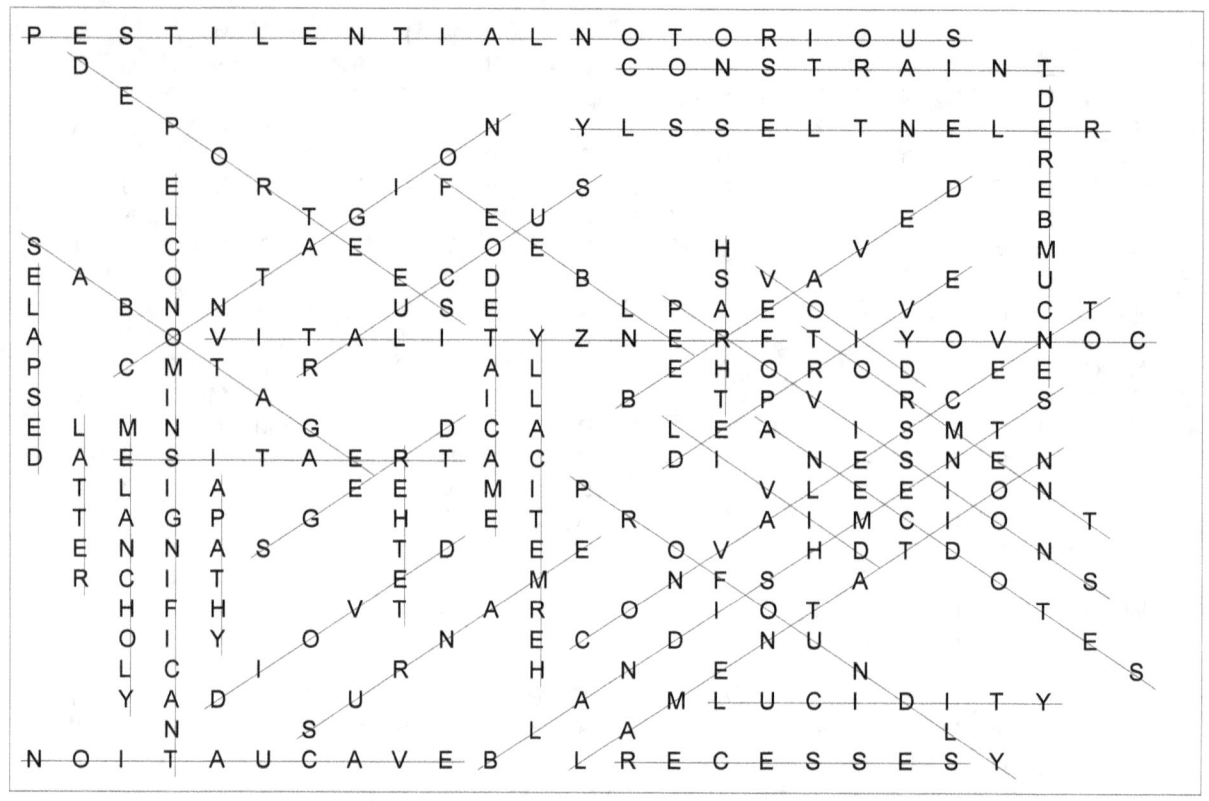

ANECDOTES	DREGS	LIVID	SABOTAGE
APATHY	ELAPSED	LUCIDITY	SURNAME
BEREAVED	EMACIATED	MELANCHOLY	TETHER
BLANDISHMENTS	ENCUMBERED	MONOCLE	THRASH
CONSTRAINT	EVACUATION	NOTORIOUS	TORMENT
CONTAGION	FEEBLE	PESTILENTIAL	TREATISE
CONVALESCENT	FRENZY	PROFOUNDLY	VITALITY
CONVOY	HERMETICALLY	PROVISIONS	VOID
DEPORTEES	INSIGNIFICANT	RAUCOUS	
DEPRIVE	LAMENTATION	RECESSES	
DEVOID	LATTER	RELENTLESSLY	

Night Vocabulary Crossword 1

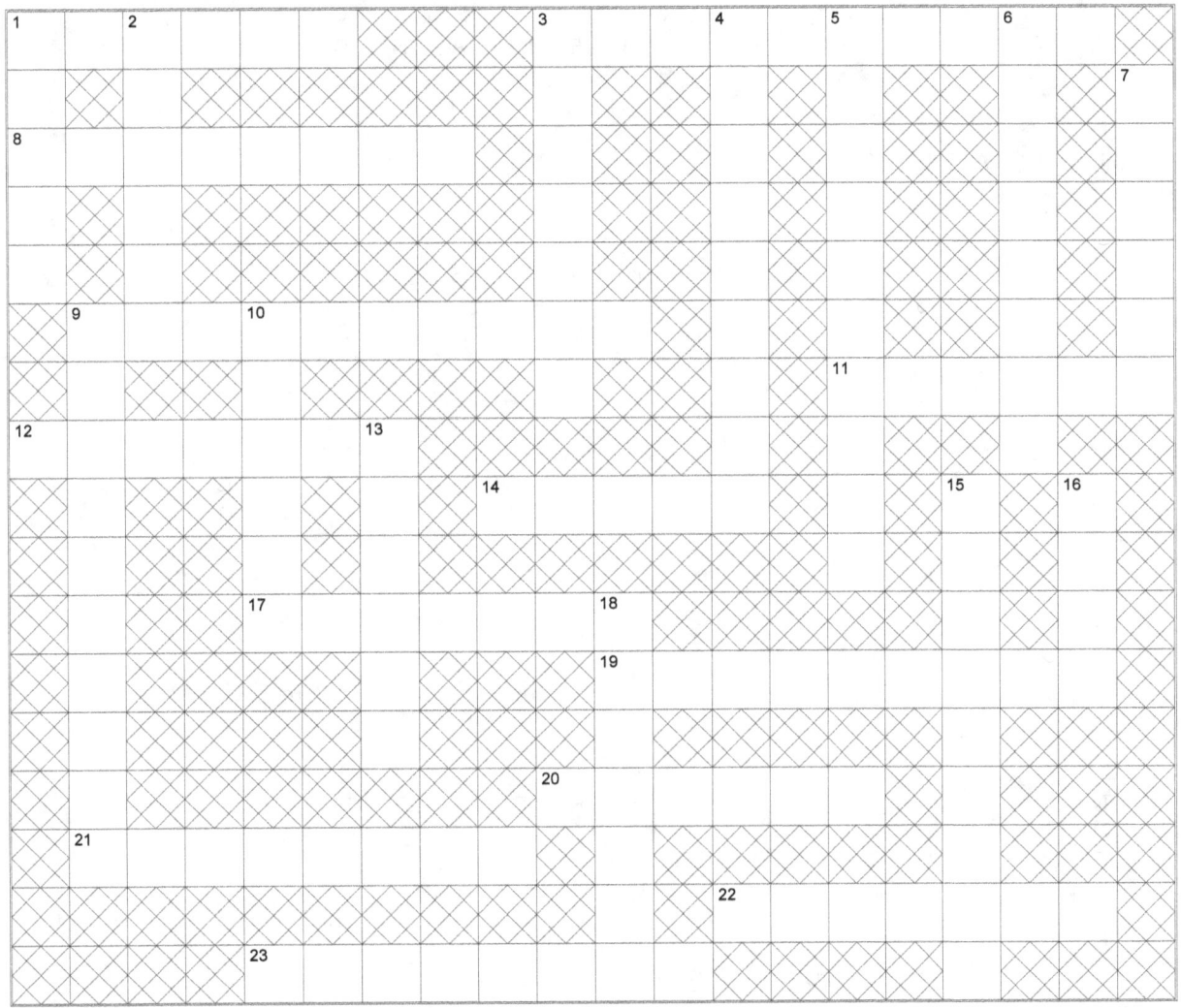

Across
1. Second of two
3. Sadness; depression
8. Vigor; energy
9. Absolutely; in an unqualified way
11. Lack of emotion or feeling
12. To cause physical pain or mental anguish
14. The least desirable portions
17. Passed
19. Made thin due to starvation
20. Violent mental agitation or wild excitement
21. Treacherous action to defeat a cause
22. Boisterous and disorderly
23. Remote, secret places

Down
1. Ashen; pallid
2. The limit of one's resources or endurance
3. An eyeglass for one eye
4. Short, humorous stories
5. Restriction
6. Clear understanding
7. A group of vehicles traveling together
9. Necessary supplies, such as food
10. Lacking strength
13. Beat; hit
15. A harmful influence
16. Emptiness
18. To take something away from

Night Vocabulary Crossword 1 Answer Key

	1 L	2 A	T	T	E	R		3 M	E	L	4 A	N	5 C	H	6 O	L	Y	
	I	E						O			N		O		U		7 C
8 V	I	T	A	L	I	T	Y		N			E		N			C	O
	I	H						O			C		S		I		N
	D	E						C			D		T		D		V
		9 P	R	O	10 F	O	U	N	D	L	Y		O		R		I	O
		R			E						E		T		11 A	P	A	T	H	Y
12 T	O	R	M	E	N	13 T						E		I			Y	
		V			B	H		14 D	R	E	G	S			15 C		16 V	
		I			L	R							T		O		O	
		17 S	E	L	A	P	S	E	18 D						N		I	
		I			S				19 E	M	A	C	I	A	T	E	D	
		O			H				P					A				
		N						20 F	R	E	N	Z	Y		G			
		21 S	A	B	O	T	A	G	E				I			I		
								I				22 R	A	U	C	O	U	S
				23 R	E	C	E	S	S	E	S				N			

Across
1. Second of two
3. Sadness; depression
8. Vigor; energy
9. Absolutely; in an unqualified way
11. Lack of emotion or feeling
12. To cause physical pain or mental anguish
14. The least desirable portions
17. Passed
19. Made thin due to starvation
20. Violent mental agitation or wild excitement
21. Treacherous action to defeat a cause
22. Boisterous and disorderly
23. Remote, secret places

Down
1. Ashen; pallid
2. The limit of one's resources or endurance
3. An eyeglass for one eye
4. Short, humorous stories
5. Restriction
6. Clear understanding
7. A group of vehicles traveling together
9. Necessary supplies, such as food
10. Lacking strength
13. Beat; hit
15. A harmful influence
16. Emptiness
18. To take something away from

Night Vocabulary Crossword 2

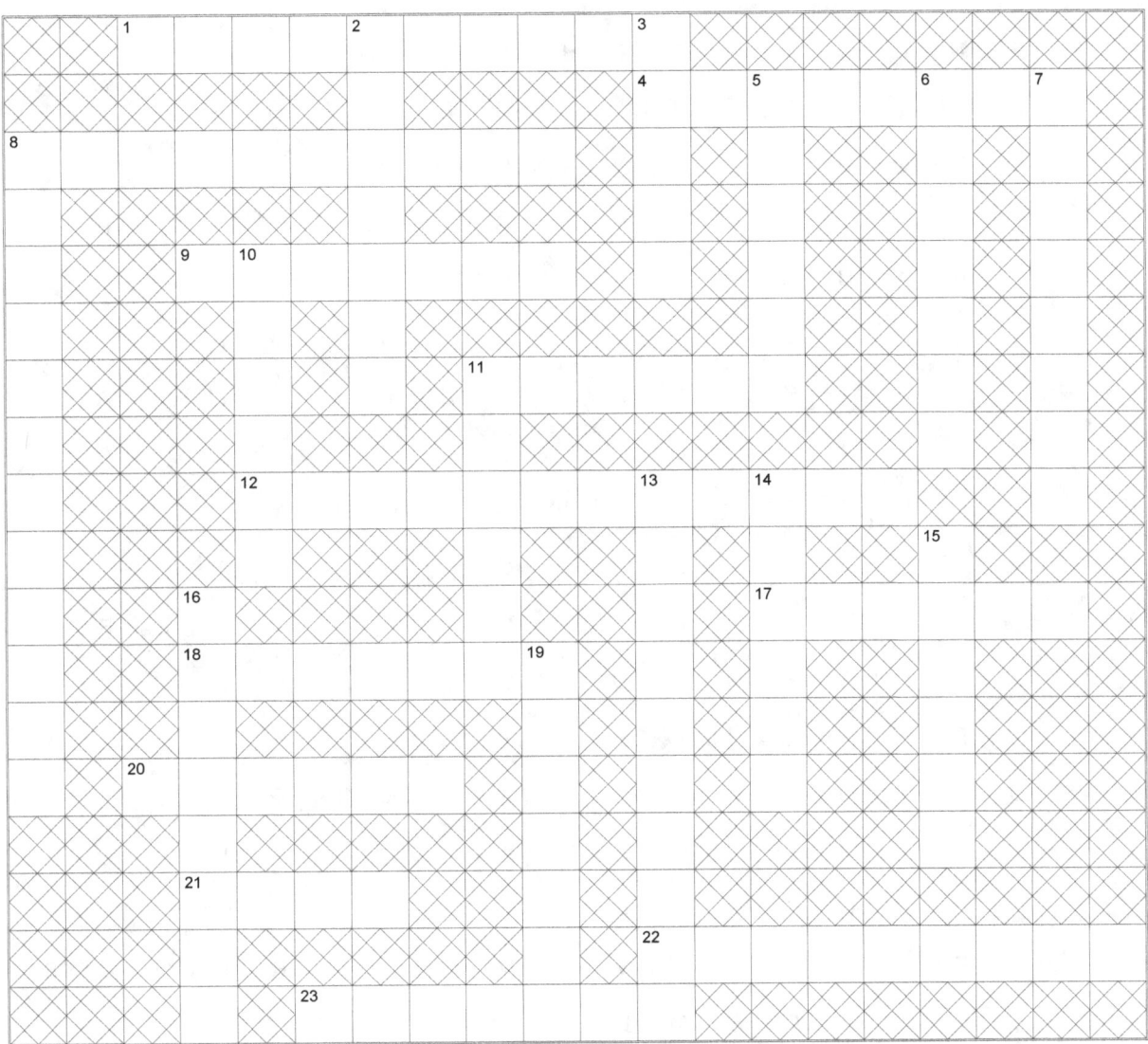

Across
1. Hindered; restricted
4. Remote, secret places
8. Absolutely; in an unqualified way
9. Boisterous and disorderly
11. Violent mental agitation or wild excitement
12. Sealed against the entry or escape of air
17. The limit of one's resources or endurance
18. Passed
20. Completely lacking or empty
21. Emptiness
22. Known unfavorably
23. To cause physical pain or mental anguish

Down
2. An eyeglass for one eye
3. The least desirable portions
5. A group of vehicles traveling together
6. Family name
7. Treacherous action to defeat a cause
8. Likely to cause an epidemic disease
10. Lack of emotion or feeling
11. Lacking strength
13. Restriction
14. Second of two
15. Beat; hit
16. Left alone by death
19. To take something away from

Night Vocabulary Crossword 2 Answer Key

Across
1. Hindered; restricted
4. Remote, secret places
8. Absolutely; in an unqualified way
9. Boisterous and disorderly
11. Violent mental agitation or wild excitement
12. Sealed against the entry or escape of air
17. The limit of one's resources or endurance
18. Passed
20. Completely lacking or empty
21. Emptiness
22. Known unfavorably
23. To cause physical pain or mental anguish

Down
2. An eyeglass for one eye
3. The least desirable portions
5. A group of vehicles traveling together
6. Family name
7. Treacherous action to defeat a cause
8. Likely to cause an epidemic disease
10. Lack of emotion or feeling
11. Lacking strength
13. Restriction
14. Second of two
15. Beat; hit
16. Left alone by death
19. To take something away from

Night Vocabulary Crossword 3

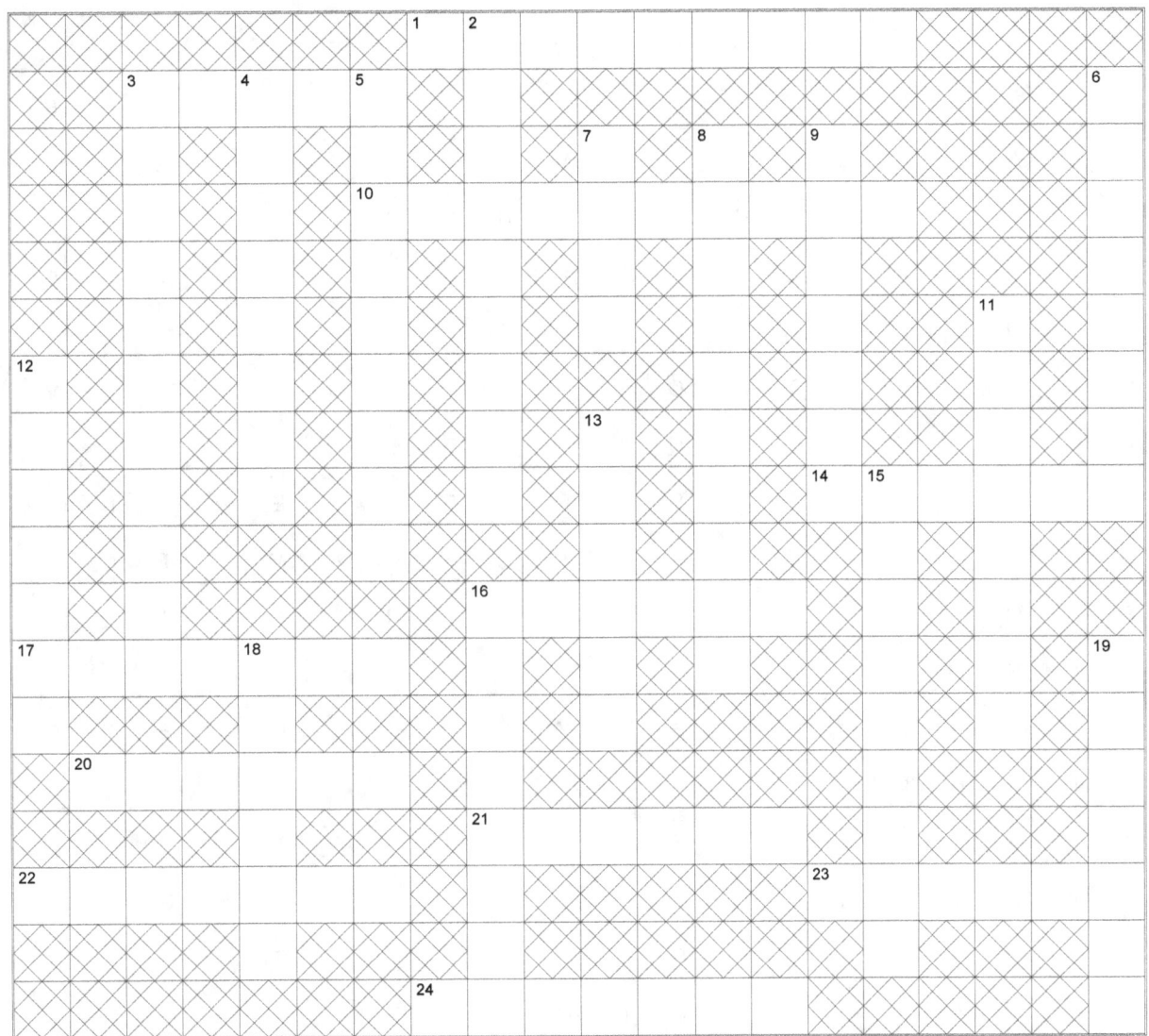

Across
1. Short, humorous stories
3. Ashen; pallid
10. Absolutely; in an unqualified way
14. Completely lacking or empty
16. The limit of one's resources or endurance
17. An eyeglass for one eye
20. Violent mental agitation or wild excitement
21. Beat; hit
22. Boisterous and disorderly
23. Lacking strength
24. To take something away from

Down
2. Known unfavorably
3. Grief; mourning
4. Vigor; energy
5. Those being expelled from a country
6. Left alone by death
7. Emptiness
8. Hindered; restricted
9. Passed
11. Treacherous action to defeat a cause
12. Family name
13. Lack of emotion or feeling
15. Made thin due to starvation
16. Written discussion of a topic
18. A group of vehicles traveling together
19. To cause physical pain or mental anguish

Night Vocabulary Crossword 3 Answer Key

```
            1  2
            A  N  E  C  D  O  T  E  S
      3  4  5
      L  I  V  I  D        O                                  6
                                                              B
         A  I  E        7     8     9
                        V     E     E                         E
                  10
         M  T     P  R  O  F  O  U  N  D  L  Y                R
         E     A     O     R  I     C     A                   E
                                                        11
         N     L     R     I     D  U     P              S    A
   12
   S     T     I     T     O        M     S              A    V
   U     A     T     E     U     13 A  B  E           14 B 15 E
   R     T     Y     E     S        P  E              D  E  V  O  I  D
   N     I           S              A  R              M     T
   A     O                       16 T  E  T  H  E  R  A     A
17          18
   M  O  N  O  C  L  E           R        H  D        C     G    19 T
   E           O                 E        Y           I     E       O
      20
      F  R  E  N  Z  Y           A                    A             R
                              21
                                 T  H  R  A  S  H     T             M
   22                                              23
   R  A  U  C  O  U  S           I                    F  E  E  B  L  E
            Y                    S                    D             N
                              24
                                 D  E  P  R  I  V  E                T
```

Across
1. Short, humorous stories
3. Ashen; pallid
10. Absolutely; in an unqualified way
14. Completely lacking or empty
16. The limit of one's resources or endurance
17. An eyeglass for one eye
20. Violent mental agitation or wild excitement
21. Beat; hit
22. Boisterous and disorderly
23. Lacking strength
24. To take something away from

Down
2. Known unfavorably
3. Grief; mourning
4. Vigor; energy
5. Those being expelled from a country
6. Left alone by death
7. Emptiness
8. Hindered; restricted
9. Passed
11. Treacherous action to defeat a cause
12. Family name
13. Lack of emotion or feeling
15. Made thin due to starvation
16. Written discussion of a topic
18. A group of vehicles traveling together
19. To cause physical pain or mental anguish

Night Vocabulary Crossword 4

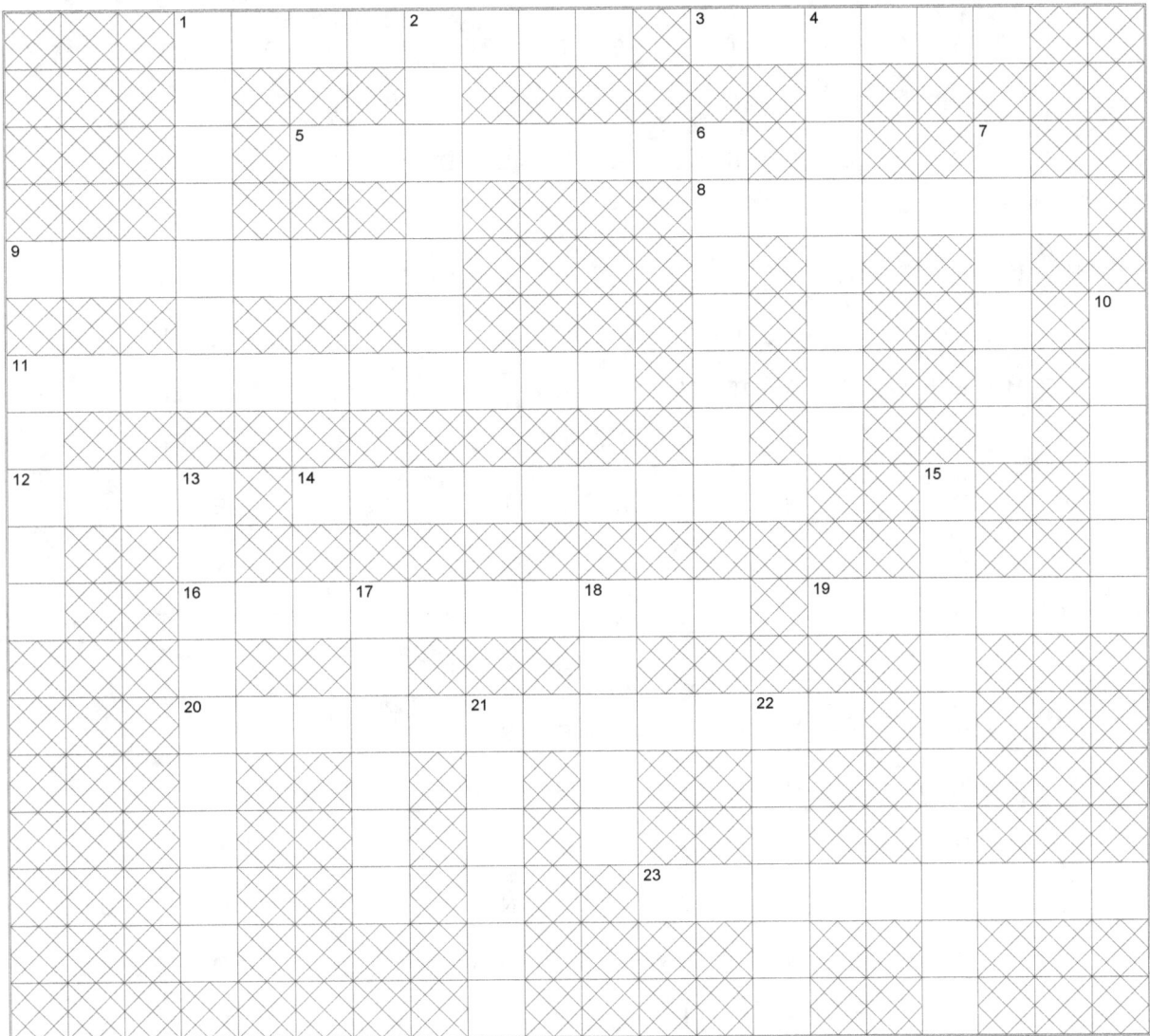

Across
1. Treacherous action to defeat a cause
3. Completely lacking or empty
5. Left alone by death
8. Passed
9. Written discussion of a topic
11. Grief; mourning
12. Emptiness
14. Short, humorous stories
16. Absolutely; in an unqualified way
19. Lack of emotion or feeling
20. Steadily; persistently
23. Known unfavorably

Down
1. Family name
2. To cause physical pain or mental anguish
4. Vigor; energy
6. To take something away from
7. The limit of one's resources or endurance
10. A group of vehicles traveling together
11. Ashen; pallid
13. Those being expelled from a country
15. Withdrawing troops or civilians from an area
17. Violent mental agitation or wild excitement
18. The least desirable portions
21. Beat; hit
22. Second of two

Night Vocabulary Crossword 4 Answer Key

Across
1. Treacherous action to defeat a cause
3. Completely lacking or empty
5. Left alone by death
8. Passed
9. Written discussion of a topic
11. Grief; mourning
12. Emptiness
14. Short, humorous stories
16. Absolutely; in an unqualified way
19. Lack of emotion or feeling
20. Steadily; persistently
23. Known unfavorably

Down
1. Family name
2. To cause physical pain or mental anguish
4. Vigor; energy
6. To take something away from
7. The limit of one's resources or endurance
10. A group of vehicles traveling together
11. Ashen; pallid
13. Those being expelled from a country
15. Withdrawing troops or civilians from an area
17. Violent mental agitation or wild excitement
18. The least desirable portions
21. Beat; hit
22. Second of two

Night Vocabulary Juggle Letters 1

1. RDVIEEP = 1. _____
To take something away from

2. SCUAURO = 2. _____
Boisterous and disorderly

3. HASRTH = 3. _____
Beat; hit

4. EDMCEEUNBR = 4. _____
Hindered; restricted

5. DOIV = 5. _____
Emptiness

6. RTCNNOASIT = 6. _____
Restriction

7. AITMCEEDA = 7. _____
Made thin due to starvation

8. OECOMLN = 8. _____
An eyeglass for one eye

9. LREEYLCTMIAH = 9. _____
Sealed against the entry or escape of air

10. ANICTEOVAU =10. _____
Withdrawing troops or civilians from an area

11. OVCNOY =11. _____
A group of vehicles traveling together

12. HTAYAP =12. _____
Lack of emotion or feeling

13. NELSELYRTESL =13. _____
Steadily; persistently

14. TLMOANAETNI =14. _____
Grief; mourning

15. AOGCNTINO =15. _____
A harmful influence

Copyrighted

Night Vocabulary Juggle Letters 1 Answer Key

1. RDVIEEP = 1. DEPRIVE
   To take something away from

2. SCUAURO = 2. RAUCOUS
   Boisterous and disorderly

3. HASRTH = 3. THRASH
   Beat; hit

4. EDMCEEUNBR = 4. ENCUMBERED
   Hindered; restricted

5. DOIV = 5. VOID
   Emptiness

6. RTCNNOASIT = 6. CONSTRAINT
   Restriction

7. AITMCEEDA = 7. EMACIATED
   Made thin due to starvation

8. OECOMLN = 8. MONOCLE
   An eyeglass for one eye

9. LREEYLCTMIAH = 9. HERMETICALLY
   Sealed against the entry or escape of air

10. ANICTEOVAU = 10. EVACUATION
    Withdrawing troops or civilians from an area

11. OVCNOY = 11. CONVOY
    A group of vehicles traveling together

12. HTAYAP = 12. APATHY
    Lack of emotion or feeling

13. NELSELYRTESL = 13. RELENTLESSLY
    Steadily; persistently

14. TLMOANAETNI = 14. LAMENTATION
    Grief; mourning

15. AOGCNTINO = 15. CONTAGION
    A harmful influence

Night Vocabulary Juggle Letters 2

1. BEFELE = 1. _____
Lacking strength

2. AESEPDL = 2. _____
Passed

3. HRTSHA = 3. _____
Beat; hit

4. NOMLECO = 4. _____
An eyeglass for one eye

5. EEBERVDA = 5. _____
Left alone by death

6. DEVOID = 6. _____
Completely lacking or empty

7. NEMTROT = 7. _____
To cause physical pain or mental anguish

8. IVPOSROSIN = 8. _____
Necessary supplies, such as food

9. TALERT = 9. _____
Second of two

10. DCONSEAET = 10. _____
Short, humorous stories

11. PTYAAH = 11. _____
Lack of emotion or feeling

12. NCOVOY = 12. _____
A group of vehicles traveling together

13. IDLIV = 13. _____
Ashen; pallid

14. ITNARTSNOC = 14. _____
Restriction

15. NLTRSLEYSELE = 15. _____
Steadily; persistently

Night Vocabulary Juggle Letters 2 Answer Key

1. BEFELE = 1. FEEBLE
Lacking strength

2. AESEPDL = 2. ELAPSED
Passed

3. HRTSHA = 3. THRASH
Beat; hit

4. NOMLECO = 4. MONOCLE
An eyeglass for one eye

5. EEBERVDA = 5. BEREAVED
Left alone by death

6. DEVOID = 6. DEVOID
Completely lacking or empty

7. NEMTROT = 7. TORMENT
To cause physical pain or mental anguish

8. IVPOSROSIN = 8. PROVISIONS
Necessary supplies, such as food

9. TALERT = 9. LATTER
Second of two

10. DCONSEAET =10. ANECDOTES
Short, humorous stories

11. PTYAAH =11. APATHY
Lack of emotion or feeling

12. NCOVOY =12. CONVOY
A group of vehicles traveling together

13. IDLIV =13. LIVID
Ashen; pallid

14. ITNARTSNOC =14. CONSTRAINT
Restriction

15. NLTRSLEYSELE =15. RELENTLESSLY
Steadily; persistently

Night Vocabulary Juggle Letters 3

1. OVELACENSTNC = 1. _____
Returning to health after an illness

2. REHTTE = 2. _____
The limit of one's resources or endurance

3. EDSPEOTRE = 3. _____
Those being expelled from a country

4. YMENCOALLH = 4. _____
Sadness; depression

5. ITOMETNLANA = 5. _____
Grief; mourning

6. TANCNOGIO = 6. _____
A harmful influence

7. DEATCIEAM = 7. _____
Made thin due to starvation

8. ONUOSRITO = 8. _____
Known unfavorably

9. ONSINCTART = 9. _____
Restriction

10. IILVD =10. _____
Ashen; pallid

11. RAHHST =11. _____
Beat; hit

12. SLTMADNNISEHB =12. _____
Coaxing by flattery

13. ODEVID =13. _____
Completely lacking or empty

14. OTMERTN =14. _____
To cause physical pain or mental anguish

15. LSERTEYLLNES =15. _____
Steadily; persistently

Night Vocabulary Juggle Letters 3 Answer Key

1. OVELACENSTNC = 1. CONVALESCENT
   Returning to health after an illness

2. REHTTE = 2. TETHER
   The limit of one's resources or endurance

3. EDSPEOTRE = 3. DEPORTEES
   Those being expelled from a country

4. YMENCOALLH = 4. MELANCHOLY
   Sadness; depression

5. ITOMETNLANA = 5. LAMENTATION
   Grief; mourning

6. TANCNOGIO = 6. CONTAGION
   A harmful influence

7. DEATCIEAM = 7. EMACIATED
   Made thin due to starvation

8. ONUOSRITO = 8. NOTORIOUS
   Known unfavorably

9. ONSINCTART = 9. CONSTRAINT
   Restriction

10. IILVD = 10. LIVID
    Ashen; pallid

11. RAHHST = 11. THRASH
    Beat; hit

12. SLTMADNNISEHB = 12. BLANDISHMENTS
    Coaxing by flattery

13. ODEVID = 13. DEVOID
    Completely lacking or empty

14. OTMERTN = 14. TORMENT
    To cause physical pain or mental anguish

15. LSERTEYLLNES = 15. RELENTLESSLY
    Steadily; persistently

Night Vocabulary Juggle Letters 4

1. ARNMSUE = 1. _____
Family name

2. UFDNRYLPOO = 2. _____
Absolutely; in an unqualified way

3. NINFSGNIICTAI = 3. _____
Trivial; not important

4. NOCNTRTSIA = 4. _____
Restriction

5. AITYLVIT = 5. _____
Vigor; energy

6. ROPSNOVIIS = 6. _____
Necessary supplies, such as food

7. INNHALSBSTMED = 7. _____
Coaxing by flattery

8. ETRHTE = 8. _____
The limit of one's resources or endurance

9. OMLNOCE = 9. _____
An eyeglass for one eye

10. NGTCIAONO =10. _____
A harmful influence

11. EBDREVEA =11. _____
Left alone by death

12. ELHYMCLTEARI =12. _____
Sealed against the entry or escape of air

13. OVDI =13. _____
Emptiness

14. LVIID =14. _____
Ashen; pallid

15. EEOSPDTER =15. _____
Those being expelled from a country

Night Vocabulary Juggle Letters 4 Answer Key

1. ARNMSUE = 1. SURNAME
Family name

2. UFDNRYLPOO = 2. PROFOUNDLY
Absolutely; in an unqualified way

3. NINFSGNIICTAI = 3. INSIGNIFICANT
Trivial; not important

4. NOCNTRTSIA = 4. CONSTRAINT
Restriction

5. AITYLVIT = 5. VITALITY
Vigor; energy

6. ROPSNOVIIS = 6. PROVISIONS
Necessary supplies, such as food

7. INNHALSBSTMED = 7. BLANDISHMENTS
Coaxing by flattery

8. ETRHTE = 8. TETHER
The limit of one's resources or endurance

9. OMLNOCE = 9. MONOCLE
An eyeglass for one eye

10. NGTCIAONO = 10. CONTAGION
A harmful influence

11. EBDREVEA = 11. BEREAVED
Left alone by death

12. ELHYMCLTEARI = 12. HERMETICALLY
Sealed against the entry or escape of air

13. OVDI = 13. VOID
Emptiness

14. LVIID = 14. LIVID
Ashen; pallid

15. EEOSPDTER = 15. DEPORTEES
Those being expelled from a country

ANECDOTES	Short, humorous stories
APATHY	Lack of emotion or feeling
BEREAVED	Left alone by death
BLANDISHMENTS	Coaxing by flattery
CONSTRAINT	Restriction
CONTAGION	A harmful influence
CONVALESCENT	Returning to health after an illness

CONVOY	A group of vehicles traveling together
DEPORTEES	Those being expelled from a country
DEPRIVE	To take something away from
DEVOID	Completely lacking or empty
DREGS	The least desirable portions
ELAPSED	Passed
EMACIATED	Made thin due to starvation

ENCUMBERED	Hindered; restricted
EVACUATION	Withdrawing troops or civilians from an area
FEEBLE	Lacking strength
FRENZY	Violent mental agitation or wild excitement
HERMETICALLY	Sealed against the entry or escape of air
INSIGNIFICANT	Trivial; not important
LAMENTATION	Grief; mourning

LATTER	Second of two
LIVID	Ashen; pallid
LUCIDITY	Clear understanding
MELANCHOLY	Sadness; depression
MONOCLE	An eyeglass for one eye
NOTORIOUS	Known unfavorably
PESTILENTIAL	Likely to cause an epidemic disease

PROFOUNDLY	Absolutely; in an unqualified way
PROVISIONS	Necessary supplies, such as food
RAUCOUS	Boisterous and disorderly
RECESSES	Remote, secret places
RELENTLESSLY	Steadily; persistently
SABOTAGE	Treacherous action to defeat a cause
SURNAME	Family name

TETHER	The limit of one's resources or endurance
THRASH	Beat; hit
TORMENT	To cause physical pain or mental anguish
TREATISE	Written discussion of a topic
VITALITY	Vigor; energy
VOID	Emptiness

Night Vocabulary

TETHER	CONSTRAINT	SABOTAGE	SURNAME	ANECDOTES
HERMETICALLY	BEREAVED	NOTORIOUS	PESTILENTIAL	RELENTLESSLY
ENCUMBERED	TREATISE	FREE SPACE	PROVISIONS	CONVALESCENT
RAUCOUS	THRASH	CONTAGION	VITALITY	LATTER
INSIGNIFICANT	EMACIATED	CONVOY	FRENZY	ELAPSED

Night Vocabulary

APATHY	FEEBLE	DEVOID	BLANDISHMENTS	RECESSES
DEPRIVE	LUCIDITY	DEPORTEES	TORMENT	DREGS
MONOCLE	VOID	FREE SPACE	EVACUATION	LIVID
MELANCHOLY	ELAPSED	FRENZY	CONVOY	EMACIATED
INSIGNIFICANT	LATTER	VITALITY	CONTAGION	THRASH

Night Vocabulary

SABOTAGE	VOID	EVACUATION	NOTORIOUS	LUCIDITY
RAUCOUS	ELAPSED	DEPORTEES	DEPRIVE	SURNAME
FRENZY	MONOCLE	FREE SPACE	TREATISE	FEEBLE
CONVALESCENT	PROFOUNDLY	TORMENT	RECESSES	LIVID
BLANDISHMENTS	HERMETICALLY	RELENTLESSLY	DEVOID	DREGS

Night Vocabulary

TETHER	APATHY	VITALITY	ENCUMBERED	LAMENTATION
PROVISIONS	EMACIATED	PESTILENTIAL	LATTER	CONTAGION
INSIGNIFICANT	MELANCHOLY	FREE SPACE	BEREAVED	CONVOY
THRASH	DREGS	DEVOID	RELENTLESSLY	HERMETICALLY
BLANDISHMENTS	LIVID	RECESSES	TORMENT	PROFOUNDLY

Night Vocabulary

TETHER	DEPRIVE	BLANDISHMENTS	DREGS	EVACUATION
CONTAGION	TORMENT	PROVISIONS	RAUCOUS	LATTER
INSIGNIFICANT	THRASH	FREE SPACE	SABOTAGE	PROFOUNDLY
PESTILENTIAL	TREATISE	HERMETICALLY	VOID	SURNAME
FEEBLE	CONVALESCENT	DEPORTEES	LUCIDITY	CONSTRAINT

Night Vocabulary

VITALITY	EMACIATED	CONVOY	LIVID	RELENTLESSLY
ENCUMBERED	MONOCLE	FRENZY	NOTORIOUS	ANECDOTES
LAMENTATION	ELAPSED	FREE SPACE	DEVOID	BEREAVED
RECESSES	CONSTRAINT	LUCIDITY	DEPORTEES	CONVALESCENT
FEEBLE	SURNAME	VOID	HERMETICALLY	TREATISE

Night Vocabulary

CONVALESCENT	DEVOID	EVACUATION	FRENZY	HERMETICALLY
LATTER	PROFOUNDLY	DREGS	ELAPSED	BLANDISHMENTS
ENCUMBERED	RECESSES	FREE SPACE	THRASH	FEEBLE
VITALITY	TREATISE	PESTILENTIAL	TORMENT	SABOTAGE
SURNAME	DEPRIVE	PROVISIONS	APATHY	CONVOY

Night Vocabulary

VOID	CONSTRAINT	INSIGNIFICANT	LUCIDITY	MONOCLE
EMACIATED	LAMENTATION	RAUCOUS	CONTAGION	NOTORIOUS
TETHER	RELENTLESSLY	FREE SPACE	ANECDOTES	DEPORTEES
MELANCHOLY	CONVOY	APATHY	PROVISIONS	DEPRIVE
SURNAME	SABOTAGE	TORMENT	PESTILENTIAL	TREATISE

Night Vocabulary

LIVID	TORMENT	LUCIDITY	CONVOY	SABOTAGE
CONTAGION	ANECDOTES	FEEBLE	THRASH	BLANDISHMENTS
APATHY	NOTORIOUS	FREE SPACE	RELENTLESSLY	TETHER
PROFOUNDLY	BEREAVED	MELANCHOLY	ENCUMBERED	LAMENTATION
HERMETICALLY	RAUCOUS	RECESSES	CONVALESCENT	PESTILENTIAL

Night Vocabulary

PROVISIONS	DEPRIVE	EMACIATED	LATTER	VITALITY
DEVOID	CONSTRAINT	MONOCLE	ELAPSED	VOID
TREATISE	INSIGNIFICANT	FREE SPACE	DREGS	EVACUATION
SURNAME	PESTILENTIAL	CONVALESCENT	RECESSES	RAUCOUS
HERMETICALLY	LAMENTATION	ENCUMBERED	MELANCHOLY	BEREAVED

Night Vocabulary

CONTAGION	PROFOUNDLY	TETHER	DEPORTEES	VOID
RELENTLESSLY	EMACIATED	CONVOY	BEREAVED	RECESSES
HERMETICALLY	PROVISIONS	FREE SPACE	INSIGNIFICANT	SURNAME
NOTORIOUS	DEPRIVE	CONVALESCENT	ENCUMBERED	RAUCOUS
BLANDISHMENTS	MONOCLE	TORMENT	DEVOID	LUCIDITY

Night Vocabulary

THRASH	TREATISE	VITALITY	CONSTRAINT	PESTILENTIAL
FEEBLE	DREGS	EVACUATION	APATHY	ANECDOTES
LAMENTATION	MELANCHOLY	FREE SPACE	LIVID	LATTER
FRENZY	LUCIDITY	DEVOID	TORMENT	MONOCLE
BLANDISHMENTS	RAUCOUS	ENCUMBERED	CONVALESCENT	DEPRIVE

Night Vocabulary

MELANCHOLY	LAMENTATION	PESTILENTIAL	ENCUMBERED	DEVOID
INSIGNIFICANT	FRENZY	SABOTAGE	DEPORTEES	VITALITY
SURNAME	THRASH	FREE SPACE	VOID	RELENTLESSLY
PROVISIONS	LIVID	CONVALESCENT	EVACUATION	PROFOUNDLY
TETHER	FEEBLE	CONSTRAINT	ANECDOTES	DEPRIVE

Night Vocabulary

NOTORIOUS	LUCIDITY	TORMENT	CONVOY	TREATISE
CONTAGION	APATHY	BLANDISHMENTS	HERMETICALLY	LATTER
MONOCLE	EMACIATED	FREE SPACE	RAUCOUS	DREGS
RECESSES	DEPRIVE	ANECDOTES	CONSTRAINT	FEEBLE
TETHER	PROFOUNDLY	EVACUATION	CONVALESCENT	LIVID

Night Vocabulary

RAUCOUS	HERMETICALLY	VOID	BLANDISHMENTS	LATTER
RELENTLESSLY	MELANCHOLY	CONSTRAINT	THRASH	SABOTAGE
CONTAGION	TETHER	FREE SPACE	RECESSES	DREGS
LIVID	CONVOY	EVACUATION	NOTORIOUS	DEVOID
CONVALESCENT	TORMENT	PROFOUNDLY	ANECDOTES	BEREAVED

Night Vocabulary

PESTILENTIAL	MONOCLE	FEEBLE	SURNAME	PROVISIONS
DEPORTEES	INSIGNIFICANT	DEPRIVE	LUCIDITY	VITALITY
ENCUMBERED	ELAPSED	FREE SPACE	APATHY	TREATISE
FRENZY	BEREAVED	ANECDOTES	PROFOUNDLY	TORMENT
CONVALESCENT	DEVOID	NOTORIOUS	EVACUATION	CONVOY

Night Vocabulary

RELENTLESSLY	CONTAGION	TREATISE	ELAPSED	DEPORTEES
SABOTAGE	SURNAME	NOTORIOUS	PESTILENTIAL	CONSTRAINT
LIVID	BLANDISHMENTS	FREE SPACE	EMACIATED	VOID
HERMETICALLY	TETHER	LATTER	TORMENT	PROFOUNDLY
RECESSES	ENCUMBERED	MONOCLE	ANECDOTES	INSIGNIFICANT

Night Vocabulary

VITALITY	BEREAVED	FEEBLE	LAMENTATION	EVACUATION
FRENZY	APATHY	RAUCOUS	CONVALESCENT	DREGS
PROVISIONS	LUCIDITY	FREE SPACE	THRASH	CONVOY
DEPRIVE	INSIGNIFICANT	ANECDOTES	MONOCLE	ENCUMBERED
RECESSES	PROFOUNDLY	TORMENT	LATTER	TETHER

Night Vocabulary

LAMENTATION	LUCIDITY	TETHER	DEPRIVE	HERMETICALLY
LATTER	RAUCOUS	INSIGNIFICANT	SURNAME	THRASH
MELANCHOLY	VITALITY	FREE SPACE	EMACIATED	CONTAGION
ENCUMBERED	RELENTLESSLY	RECESSES	ELAPSED	PROVISIONS
ANECDOTES	MONOCLE	BLANDISHMENTS	BEREAVED	PROFOUNDLY

Night Vocabulary

EVACUATION	NOTORIOUS	FRENZY	SABOTAGE	CONVALESCENT
FEEBLE	CONSTRAINT	VOID	APATHY	TREATISE
PESTILENTIAL	DREGS	FREE SPACE	DEVOID	DEPORTEES
LIVID	PROFOUNDLY	BEREAVED	BLANDISHMENTS	MONOCLE
ANECDOTES	PROVISIONS	ELAPSED	RECESSES	RELENTLESSLY

Night Vocabulary

MELANCHOLY	DEVOID	ANECDOTES	CONVOY	LIVID
RELENTLESSLY	VITALITY	CONTAGION	MONOCLE	VOID
TETHER	BEREAVED	FREE SPACE	FEEBLE	EVACUATION
INSIGNIFICANT	RECESSES	RAUCOUS	CONVALESCENT	CONSTRAINT
NOTORIOUS	TREATISE	ENCUMBERED	PROVISIONS	LUCIDITY

Night Vocabulary

LAMENTATION	BLANDISHMENTS	PESTILENTIAL	LATTER	TORMENT
HERMETICALLY	APATHY	DREGS	DEPORTEES	THRASH
FRENZY	SURNAME	FREE SPACE	ELAPSED	EMACIATED
SABOTAGE	LUCIDITY	PROVISIONS	ENCUMBERED	TREATISE
NOTORIOUS	CONSTRAINT	CONVALESCENT	RAUCOUS	RECESSES

Night Vocabulary

EMACIATED	APATHY	VOID	RELENTLESSLY	NOTORIOUS
RECESSES	PROVISIONS	LIVID	ANECDOTES	CONVALESCENT
BLANDISHMENTS	CONSTRAINT	FREE SPACE	ELAPSED	SURNAME
VITALITY	INSIGNIFICANT	MELANCHOLY	MONOCLE	HERMETICALLY
TREATISE	FRENZY	DEPRIVE	TORMENT	CONTAGION

Night Vocabulary

DREGS	TETHER	PESTILENTIAL	THRASH	DEVOID
EVACUATION	CONVOY	SABOTAGE	LAMENTATION	BEREAVED
DEPORTEES	RAUCOUS	FREE SPACE	FEEBLE	LATTER
ENCUMBERED	CONTAGION	TORMENT	DEPRIVE	FRENZY
TREATISE	HERMETICALLY	MONOCLE	MELANCHOLY	INSIGNIFICANT

Night Vocabulary

CONSTRAINT	DEVOID	FRENZY	PROFOUNDLY	RECESSES
VITALITY	EVACUATION	RELENTLESSLY	CONTAGION	PESTILENTIAL
DEPRIVE	LATTER	FREE SPACE	ELAPSED	INSIGNIFICANT
ANECDOTES	MELANCHOLY	FEEBLE	RAUCOUS	HERMETICALLY
TREATISE	ENCUMBERED	DEPORTEES	CONVOY	LAMENTATION

Night Vocabulary

THRASH	SURNAME	DREGS	VOID	APATHY
NOTORIOUS	BLANDISHMENTS	MONOCLE	BEREAVED	LUCIDITY
CONVALESCENT	PROVISIONS	FREE SPACE	TETHER	LIVID
SABOTAGE	LAMENTATION	CONVOY	DEPORTEES	ENCUMBERED
TREATISE	HERMETICALLY	RAUCOUS	FEEBLE	MELANCHOLY

Night Vocabulary

CONTAGION	LUCIDITY	EVACUATION	NOTORIOUS	TETHER
MONOCLE	TORMENT	INSIGNIFICANT	PROFOUNDLY	MELANCHOLY
BEREAVED	DREGS	FREE SPACE	DEVOID	DEPORTEES
ANECDOTES	FEEBLE	VITALITY	THRASH	APATHY
SABOTAGE	CONVOY	FRENZY	LATTER	DEPRIVE

Night Vocabulary

CONSTRAINT	EMACIATED	PROVISIONS	SURNAME	CONVALESCENT
LIVID	HERMETICALLY	RELENTLESSLY	LAMENTATION	VOID
BLANDISHMENTS	ENCUMBERED	FREE SPACE	ELAPSED	TREATISE
RAUCOUS	DEPRIVE	LATTER	FRENZY	CONVOY
SABOTAGE	APATHY	THRASH	VITALITY	FEEBLE

Night Vocabulary

ANECDOTES	LUCIDITY	RELENTLESSLY	DREGS	RAUCOUS
CONVALESCENT	LAMENTATION	BEREAVED	PROVISIONS	MONOCLE
CONVOY	NOTORIOUS	FREE SPACE	LIVID	TETHER
MELANCHOLY	RECESSES	EVACUATION	SURNAME	EMACIATED
ENCUMBERED	DEPRIVE	FRENZY	PROFOUNDLY	CONSTRAINT

Night Vocabulary

CONTAGION	DEVOID	DEPORTEES	VOID	TORMENT
VITALITY	BLANDISHMENTS	TREATISE	INSIGNIFICANT	SABOTAGE
ELAPSED	PESTILENTIAL	FREE SPACE	FEEBLE	HERMETICALLY
APATHY	CONSTRAINT	PROFOUNDLY	FRENZY	DEPRIVE
ENCUMBERED	EMACIATED	SURNAME	EVACUATION	RECESSES

Night Vocabulary

DEPRIVE	TORMENT	PESTILENTIAL	THRASH	EMACIATED
CONVOY	MELANCHOLY	PROVISIONS	SURNAME	NOTORIOUS
RELENTLESSLY	TETHER	FREE SPACE	ELAPSED	DEPORTEES
LAMENTATION	LIVID	LUCIDITY	LATTER	FEEBLE
RECESSES	PROFOUNDLY	CONSTRAINT	DEVOID	EVACUATION

Night Vocabulary

FRENZY	VITALITY	VOID	ENCUMBERED	BLANDISHMENTS
TREATISE	CONVALESCENT	ANECDOTES	APATHY	INSIGNIFICANT
SABOTAGE	DREGS	FREE SPACE	MONOCLE	CONTAGION
BEREAVED	EVACUATION	DEVOID	CONSTRAINT	PROFOUNDLY
RECESSES	FEEBLE	LATTER	LUCIDITY	LIVID

www.ingramcontent.com/pod-product-compliance
Lightning Source LLC
Chambersburg PA
CBHW081457070526
44586CB00019B/2392